A  of Alternative Governance Structures and Organizational Forms

Michael Hynes

Sheila Nataraj Kirby

Jennifer Sloan

Prepared for the
Office of the Secretary of Defense

National Defense Research Institute

RAND

Experience indicates that the corporate form of organization is peculiarly adapted to the administration of governmental programs which are (1) predominantly of a commercial character; (2) are at least potentially self-sustaining; and (3) involve a large number of business-type transactions with the public.

> Harry S. Truman, Budget Message to Congress, 1948

The federal government will not start or carry out any commercial activity to provide a service or product for its own use if such product or service can be procured from private enterprise through ordinary channels.

> Dwight D. Eisenhower, Bureau of the Budget Bulletin, 1955

Today I am taking what I hope and believe will be a historic step in reforming the federal government by announcing the formation of a national performance review. Our goal is to make the entire federal government both less expensive and more efficient and to change the culture of our national bureaucracy away from complacency and entitlement toward initiative and empowerment. We intend to redesign, to reinvent, to reinvigorate the entire national government.

> William Jefferson Clinton, Old Executive Office Building, March 3, 1993

PREFACE

RAND was approached by the Defense Reform Initiative Office and asked to conduct a short-term effort examining alternative ways that government could carry out its activities. This document reports the results of that effort. As a reference document, it should prove useful to government agencies and decisionmakers, both within and outside the Department of Defense, who are considering options for organizing themselves or their functions in different ways.

This research was sponsored by the Defense Reform Initiative Office within the Office of the Secretary of Defense, and it was carried out in the Forces and Resources Policy Center of RAND's National Defense Research Institute, a federally funded research and development center sponsored by the Office of the Secretary of Defense, the Joint Staff, the unified commands, and the defense agencies.

CONTENTS

FIGURES

TABLES

SUMMARY

Since the earliest days of the Continental Congress, our government has sought alternative organizational and procedural constructs for important government supporting functions and instruments of policy that are inherently commercial in nature. In this modern era, the need for alternatives is even more pressing as the form and nature of government requirements become increasingly complex and budgets are constrained.

Some functions by their very definition cannot be performed other than in-house. These inherently governmental functions involve the discretionary use of governmental authority or in some way commit the government to a specific course of action or financial expenditure as stated in 48 CFR 7.5. If an activity is considered commercial or it can be restructured to partition the governmental and commercial functions, competitive sourcing is usually selected to allow the in-house group to participate in the competitive process. Additional tests to determine whether an activity is commercial or governmental are in OMB Circular A-76.

In this report, we consider governance structures and organizational forms that offer alternatives to the usual in-house provision of services. These alternatives often offer a chance to adopt modern business practices, streamline the organization, and adopt market mechanisms to improve quality, lower costs, and become more responsive to constituencies. The alternatives considered here have a wide variety of characteristics. We found it useful to array them along the dimension of ownership of process and customer base. These range from totally governmental to totally private or somewhere in between. In addition, we also consider a number of other characteristics that distinguish these alternatives from one another. These are summarized in a table that is helpful as an organizing framework and as a way to select an appropriate choice set of alternatives for a given function or activity. The suitability of any alternative clearly depends on the specific goals of the effort and the contextual details of the situation under consideration. To illustrate some of these specifics, the main body of the report briefly describes the important features of the alternatives and one or more case studies that illustrate the application of the alternative.

ACKNOWLEDGMENTS

We are grateful to our project sponsor, Mary Margaret Evans, for her interest in and support of the study. We thank our RAND colleagues, Frank Camm and Al Robbert, who reviewed the draft report and provided us with detailed and thoughtful comments. The report has benefited considerably from their comments in terms of both substance and clarity. We also had several useful discussions with Frank Camm regarding the organization of the material and the appendix on competitive sourcing. Susan Gates, another RAND colleague, and Susan Hosek, our program director, also provided helpful comments on the draft report. We thank our editor, Patricia Bedrosian, for her patience and her skilful editing.

ACRONYMS

AETC	Air Education and Training Command
AFB	Air Force Base
AFMC	Air Force Materiel Command
AGMC	Aerospace Guidance and Metrology Center
API	Amelang Partners, Inc.
AVLIS	Atomic Vapor Laser Isotope Separation
BAA	British Airport Authority
BGRC	Boeing Guidance Repair Center
BOS	Base Operating Support
BRAC	Base Realignment and Closure Commission
CAMIS	Commercial Activity Management Information System
CASU	Cooperative Administrative Support Unit
CEO	Chief Executive Officer
CFR	Code of Federal Regulations
CNA	Center for Naval Analyses
COO	Chief Operating Officer
CORM	Commission on Roles and Missions of the Armed Forces
COTS	Commercial Off-the-Shelf

CS&P	Competitive Sourcing and Privatization
DA	Direct Appropriations
DoD	Department of Defense
DoE	Department of Energy
DRI	Defense Reform Initiative
EEOC	Equal Employment Opportunity Commission
EPA	Environmental Protection Agency
ESOP	Employee Stock Ownership Plan
EUL	Enhanced-Use Lease
FAA	Federal Aviation Agency
FAR	Federal Acquisition Regulation
FEB	Federal Executive Board
FFRDC	Federally Funded Research and Development Center
FGC	Federal Government Corporation
FTE	Full-Time Equivalent
GAO	Government Accounting Office
GGNRA	Golden Gate National Recreation Area
GOCO	Government-Owned Contractor-Operated
GSA	General Services Administration
GSE	Government-Sponsored Enterprise
HEU	High Enriched Uranium
HUD	Housing and Urban Development
IDQ	Indefinite Quantity Delivery
IMC	International Marine Carriers, Inc.
IPO	Initial Public Offering
IRS	Internal Revenue Service
ISSA	Inter Service Support Agreement

JPL	Jet Propulsion Laboratory
LEU	Low Enriched Uranium
LISA	Logistics Information Systems Agency
LMI	Logistics Management Institute
MCTD	Marine Corps Training Depot
MEO	Most Efficient Organization
MOU	Memorandum of Understanding
MSC	Military Sealift Command
NASA	National Aeronautics and Space Administration
NCO	Noncommissioned Officer
NDRI	National Defense Research Institute
NFC	National Finance Center
NRO	National Reconnaissance Office
NYSE	New York Stock Exchange
O&P	Outsourcing and Privatization
OMB	Office of Management and Budget
OPM	Office of Personnel Management
OSD	Office of the Secretary of Defense
OSFAP	Office of Student Financial Assistance Programs
OSHA	Occupational Safety and Health Administration
PBO	Performance-Based Organization
PWS	Performance Work Statement
QA	Quality Assurance
RCA	Rincon Center Associates
RDX	Royal Demolition Explosives
RFP	Request for Proposal
RFQ	Request for Qualification

SBA	Small Business Administration
SCORE	Service Corps of Retired Executives
SEC	Securities and Exchange Commission
SFAP	Student Financial Aid Program
SMC	Space and Missile Systems Center
UPS	United Parcel Service
USDA	U.S. Department of Agriculture
USEC	United States Enrichment Corporation
USIS	U.S. Investigative Services
USPS	U.S. Postal Service
VA	Veterans Affairs
VAMC	VA Medical Center

Chapter One

OVERVIEW

As the quotes from Truman, Eisenhower, and Clinton in the Foreword of this report all indicate, our government has been reinventing itself for many years. Indeed, from the earliest days of the Continental Congress, it was recognized that some functions are better performed by a commercial organization outside the government. In 1781, the Continental Congress chartered the Bank of North America to handle the finances of the emerging nation and purchased 60 percent of its shares. At that time it was felt that a colonial bank would handle the financial affairs of the colonies better than the British banks. This first government corporation insulated the nation's finances from the vagaries of both national and international politics while still allowing a high level of governmental control. Even then, the Continental Congress was concerned about the inefficiency of government and appointed an Inspector General whose charter was to "root out abuses which prevail in different departments."

The Progressive Movement in public administration (1890–1910) foreshadowed the current era in its emphasis on making government more businesslike and eliminating administrative discretion. The basic underlying tenet of its philosophy was that there was one best way to handle a given situation and all these "best practices" could be captured in a rule book. Unfortunately, in the current era, the negative aspects of the Progressive approach have become apparent—government is beset with too many rules and not enough flexibility in adapting to a rapidly changing world. The most successful business organizations of today are respected for their capacity to innovate by learning and adapting to new and changing environments, technology, and know-how while at the same time remaining

1

responsive to the needs of their customers and clients. These modern business-like themes are echoed in the current era in the National Partnership for Reinventing Government and more directly in the Department of Defense (DoD) by the Defense Reform Initiative (DRI). In November 1997, Secretary Cohen introduced the DRI in an effort to oversee reform initiatives within the department, to coordinate DoD's initiatives with those being undertaken outside the department, and to foster "a revolution in business affairs within DoD that will bring to the Department techniques and business practices that have restored American corporations to leadership in the marketplace" (Defense Reform Initiative, 1997).

DoD is in the process of examining traditional ways of doing business and increasingly looking to competition as the way to make departmental agencies and support structures more agile and efficient. The National Defense Research Institute was asked to undertake a two-month study of the range of options available to DoD in terms of alternative ways of doing business and to provide some useful case studies that would illustrate each option. This report is the result of that short-term effort.

ORGANIZATION OF THE REPORT

The main body of the report first profiles each alternative in terms of its ownership, staffing, customers, cash flow, and pros and cons. Each alternative is illustrated by one or more brief case studies that focus on implementation, major facilitating and constraining factors, and results. This section provides a brief overview of the various alternatives considered in this report. Because of the considerable interest in competitive sourcing as a way to make the government more cost-effective and efficient, the appendix provides a brief discussion of some issues related to competitive sourcing. Following the appendix is a glossary of terms related to privatization used by the U.S. Government Accounting Office (GAO)[1] (U.S. GAO, 1997a) that may prove to be a handy reference in distinguishing among the various alternatives being discussed.

---

[1]GAO's definitions may not always be the same as those used by DoD.

INHERENTLY GOVERNMENTAL VERSUS COMMERCIAL ACTIVITIES

Some functions are proscribed from being performed by other than in-house government personnel. Title 48 defines inherently governmental functions as those that are "so intimately related to the public interest as to mandate performance by Government employees," although the regulation is careful to point out that this is a policy determination, not a legal determination (Code of Federal Regulations (CFR) Title 48). An inherently governmental function includes any activity that requires the exercise of discretion or the making of value judgments in applying government authority (48 CFR 7 Subpart 7.5).

Given that a function is not inherently governmental, various alternative ways of doing business can be considered. As we discuss below, the appropriateness of a particular alternative for a given situation depends on several characteristics including customer base, the source of funding, control over staffing, process, and outcome.[2]

---

[2]When considering efforts to privatize government activities, it is important to step back and consider the issue from a broader perspective. The underlying belief that the country's interest is best served if government becomes more like business and U.S. citizens more like customers leaves out considerable depth in the relationship between the government and the citizens (Mintzberg, 1996). Distinctions are made between inherently governmental and inherently commercial activities but do not cover a wide variety of legal issues involving Constitutional concerns such as first amendment rights, procedural and substantive due process, sovereign immunity, and the separation of powers (14 Federal Acquisition Regulation (FAR) 7, FAR Subpart 7.5 § 7.501, and Office of Management and Budget (OMB) Memorandum A-76).

A recent case before the U.S. Supreme Court highlights these concerns. In this case, Lebron claims that first amendment rights and the fifth amendment right of due process were violated by Amtrak, which, despite the fact that it is a federal corporation, acts as a branch of the government and is bound by the Constitution to deliver said rights. Amtrak, by virtue of being a corporation, claimed not to have violated any rights. The issue revolved around the federal action doctrine, which holds that "entities displaying a close relation to the government can be treated as acting for the government" and can be considered part of the government. The court opinion, written by Justice Scalia, states in part:

> It surely cannot be that government, state or federal, is able to evade the most solemn obligations imposed in the Constitution by simply resorting to the corporate form. On that thesis, *Plessy v. Ferguson* can be resurrected by the simple device of having the State of Louisiana operate segregated trains through a state-owned Amtrak.

CAVEATS

It is important to understand the limitations of this report. It presents a compendium of alternative governance structures and organizational forms, drawn from a variety of source material. Because it is a short-term effort, the descriptions and the case studies are limited to what could be drawn together in a relatively short period of time. The report does not contain any analysis or original data partly because that was not our mandate and partly because of the time constraints. Nor does the report contain guidelines that could help DoD decide among alternatives in a given situation. This would be difficult to do in the abstract, without specifying in more detail a particular case or activity to be analyzed. Even formulating general guidelines would require considerably more time and analysis than was possible in this effort. Despite these limitations, the report is a useful addition to the literature because it draws together, in one document, the spectrum of alternatives available to DoD when considering changes in the current way of doing business. It provides succinct descriptions of each, highlights differences among them, and describes case studies showing the use of the particular alternative and results of such efforts, when available.

ALTERNATIVE GOVERNANCE STRUCTURES AND ORGANIZATIONAL FORMS

This section briefly defines the alternatives considered in this report. Although we refer to them as governance structures or organizational forms, some of them are ways to transition between different governance structures.

Because the alternatives differ along a variety of dimensions, it was difficult to choose any one characteristic as the organizing principle. For simplicity, we chose to rank these alternatives according to who

---

The concern here and with several other cases is that using some of these privatization vehicles, the government—in particular Congress and the Executive Branch—could contract out of the Constitution. Other cases involve separation of powers issues associated with the retention of revenues by profitmaking government organizations in the Executive Branch in violation of the budgetary process provided for by the Congress. The application of privatization schemes requires careful consideration of the legal issues as well as the policy issues.

is providing the service. Thus, the order starts with activities provided by government organizations, followed by mixed forms—activities provided jointly by government and private organizations—and, finally, activities provided by private organizations.

Performance-Based Organizations (PBOs)

PBOs are discrete management units within a federal agency, headed by a chief operating officer (COO), who generally has a performance agreement reviewed annually. Under a PBO, policymaking is separated from service operation functions. Policymaking remains within the purview of the government department, and operational responsibility transfers to the PBO. The PBO commits to specific measurable goals, customer service standards, and targets for improved performance. A PBO remains under the full control of the government, is funded completely by the government, and is staffed by government employees. A draft Logistics Management Institute (LMI) report (Vivar and Reay, 1999) highlights some concerns:

- It may be difficult to separate policy functions from operations.

- The one-year duration of the performance agreement with the COO is too short and may provide the wrong incentives. It is important that the agency be focused on both long-term and short-term goals. The performance contract should reflect both sets of goals.

- Providing incentives to the COO is not likely to alter overall organizational behavior.

- The disruption in delivery of services during the transition may impose high costs.

Government Franchises

These administrative units of agencies provide support services to other administrative entities on a cost-reimbursable, competitive basis. Ownership remains in the hands of the government, although the units operate as self-supporting, business units. Government employees constitute the majority of the staff, but government franchises may also contract out for services. Government franchises offer some advantages: They generate revenue for the agency offering the service; for their customers, they offer lower costs and a chance to focus on core competencies.

Cooperative Partnerships

Cooperative partnerships are joint governmental initiatives in which federal, state, or local government agencies partner to provide services and information or to conduct mutual missions. Most cooperative partnerships are formed under memoranda of understanding (MOUs), although in some instances, the partners use less formal agreements. Such partnerships can help reduce or eliminate duplication of services and provide more seamless, convenient services to citizens.

Federal Government Corporations (FGCs)

There is no clear legal definition of a government corporation, and there is considerable variation among the many government corporations in existence today with respect to their structure and control. FGCs are appropriate for governmental programs or agencies that are predominantly of a business nature, produce revenue and are potentially self-sustaining, involve large numbers of business-type transactions with the public, and require greater flexibility than permitted under governmental rules (Truman, 1948). Although these criteria have been generally endorsed by several other studies, a 1996 GAO report recommended that Congress adopt a uniform definition of and standardized criteria for FGCs and strengthen oversight and accountability of them (U.S. GAO, 1996). There is some concern regarding the lack of accountability to constituencies and the potential conflicts with Constitutional issues.

Another organization—an independent establishment of the executive branch of the U.S. government—falls under the rubric of FGCs. There is only one such organization—the U.S. Postal Service (USPS)—but it essentially functions as an FGC.

Government-Owned Contractor-Operated (GOCOs)

GOCOs are a form of privatization in which the facilities and equipment are owned by the government but are operated by contractors with mostly contractor staffing. They are implemented through standard contracting methods and are entirely supported by the government. Their major advantage is their promise of efficient commercial operation of facilities for which the government is the sole customer, but concerns with oversight and control can lead to micromanagement and declines in efficiency.

Private Management

Similar to GOCOs, private management involves commercial operation of government-owned capital assets to provide a service to the public. Unlike GOCOs that supply government agencies, private management offers services to the general public. Private management offers several advantages: efficient commercial operation for the public, alternatives to public financing of facilities, and an alternative to asset sale if title is not clear. However, it also implies the potential loss of control over an important public facility and perhaps the loss of some Constitutional protections for citizen rights.

Public/Private Partnerships or Joint Ventures

In a public/private venture, public and private sector partners form a contractual agreement. Typically, under these agreements, the agency retains ownership of the public facility, the private party invests its own capital to design and develop the properties, and each partner shares in income resulting from the partnership. These shared risks and rewards distinguish public/private partnerships from the more typical contracting out of services and functions. Such joint ventures may increase efficiency and tap expertise not available in a government agency. Establishing a public/private partnership is also considerably easier than trying to dispose of property under the General Services Administration regulation.

One variant on this concept of importance to DoD is "asset financing," often used as a method of housing and utility "privatization" in

DoD.[3] These so-called privatization efforts are not what people normally mean by privatization, which is usually some form of asset sale. Rather, they cover a variety of creative ways to induce private firms to finance DoD housing and utility needs. This allows DoD to improve services without expending its own obligational authority under OMB scoring. These initiatives can be as important financially to DoD as competitive sourcing and innovative contracting in the right circumstances.

Government-Sponsored Enterprises (GSEs)

GSEs (e.g., Fannie Mae, Freddie Mac) are federally chartered but privately owned financial institutions. They are not agencies of the United States but are entities that accomplish a public purpose defined by law (i.e., enhancing the credit available to homebuyers, farmers, students, and colleges). GSEs occupy a middle ground between purely private corporations and government agencies. They benefit from implicit federal guarantees that enhance their ability to borrow money in the private market at favorable rates and to borrow from the Treasury if needed. Because they have a public purpose, some GSEs are exempt from federal, state, or local corporate income taxes and Securities and Exchange Commission registration requirements and fees. However, because they are federally chartered, they can involve significant risks to the taxpayers and have at times imposed large costs on the taxpayer.

Federally Funded Research and Development Centers (FFRDCs)

An FFRDC is created to meet a special long-term research or development need that cannot be met effectively by existing in-house or contractor resources. FFRDCs are of three basic types, providing research and development in specialized areas, policy analysis and decisionmaking support, and specialized system engineering and integration support. FFRDCs offer several advantages to their sponsoring agencies: ready access to advanced research and development capabilities, long-term relationships that foster a deeper un-

---

[3]We are grateful to our reviewer, Frank Camm, for pointing this out.

derstanding of the sponsor's priorities and problems, objectivity, and independence from partisan or ideological biases. On the minus side, they tend to be expensive and need sophisticated management to ensure that their priorities mesh with those of the sponsor.

Competitive Sourcing

Outsourcing, or competitive sourcing as it is now called, is receiving the lion's share of attention in DoD's reform efforts. It is defined as shifting functions from in-house providers to private firms, although with managed cost competitions under A-76, the in-house team may be designated as the service provider. The government remains the financier and has management and policy control over the type of quality and services to be provided. This is done using standard contracting methods but it often requires a managed cost competition. The appendix provides a detailed discussion of some issues related to competitive sourcing as well as a discussion of how to make such competitions more effective.

Employee Stock Ownership Plans (ESOPs)

Creating an ESOP is a way to privatize a previously governmental function. In an ESOP privatization, employees who were previously performing a government operation or function voluntarily form a private firm to provide the same service as private contractors. The employees receive salaries and benefits as well as dividends or a share of the profits. ESOPs are attractive as a means of privatization because of secured employment (at least in the short run), continued access to in-house expertise, enhanced productivity because employees have a direct financial stake in the performance of the company, and tax advantages. However, several concerns have been raised about ESOPs. Employees generally do not have voting rights, rarely receive dividends, have no say in the choice of a trustee, and the stocks usually form a very small portion of their compensation. Because of the rules, large functions are generally better candidates for ESOP privatization unless functions can be bundled.

Asset Sales

An asset sale is the transfer of ownership of government assets, commercial-type enterprises, or functions to the private sector. In general, the government has no role in the financial support, management, or oversight of a sold asset. However, if the asset is sold to a company in an industry with monopolistic characteristics, the government may regulate certain aspects of the business, such as utility rates.

HIGHLIGHTING DIFFERENCES AMONG ALTERNATIVES[4]

The definitions provided above, although useful in describing the spectrum of alternatives, are not very useful to a decisionmaker attempting to make decisions about appropriate alternative governance structures or organizational forms for activities or functions that are currently being carried out in house. In thinking about the characteristics that might be important to DoD, we first selected the dimension of control as the most salient characteristic. However, control itself has many dimensions and it is not easy to compress all of them into one summary indicator. For example, control could encompass any or all of the following: day-to-day operations, the design of the product or choice of process to deliver the product, staffing, physical or financial assets, and planning. In many instances, the real concern is accountability: the ability of DoD to hold the service provider accountable for the timeliness, quality, and cost of the product. However, this can be accomplished to a greater or lesser degree in almost every governance structure by putting into place appropriate incentives and performance goals. To illustrate this point, consider that accountability can be higher in a carefully executed outsourced contract than in some government departments that are hampered by civil service and other rules from levying penalties for inefficiency. In addition, many contract sources further enhance accountability by bundling, with the services they provide, cost accounting and performance measurement systems that are superior to those in the government.

---

[4]This section benefited greatly from several useful discussions with our reviewer, Frank Camm.

Therefore, we focus on dimensions that are more easily quantifiable, such as:

- Who has ownership (and, therefore, control) over the production process? This would also have some implications for staffing.
- Who are the customers for this service?

We array the set of alternatives along each of these dimensions. Clearly, however, other dimensions are important including the source of funding (direct appropriations versus sales) and the residual claimant. It is also useful to have a matrix that allows the decisionmaker to see at a glance the major similarities and distinctions among the various alternatives.

Figure 1 arrays the alternatives according to the ownership or control over the process of provision of services. We examine these from the point of view of the agency or department that is the customer for this service. Ownership of process ranges from purely governmental to purely private control. For example, the standard DoD agency controls the entire provision of services and is responsible for day-to-day operations and planning. However, PBOs and government franchises, although still remaining purely governmental in provision, are slightly removed from the more traditional department in the level of control by the department over the process. For example, government franchises involve having one department's or agency's tasks being performed by another organization in the government. Although still within the government, the process of provision is slightly less under the control of the organization receiving the services. Similarly, PBOs generally have greater flexibility in staffing and acquisition than typical government agencies or franchises, so although provision is still governmental, there is a difference in the level of ownership by the agency that is the customer. The broadest spectrum of control possibilities is demonstrated by federal government corporations, which range from mostly governmental control to mostly private control, depending on the charter of the corporation.

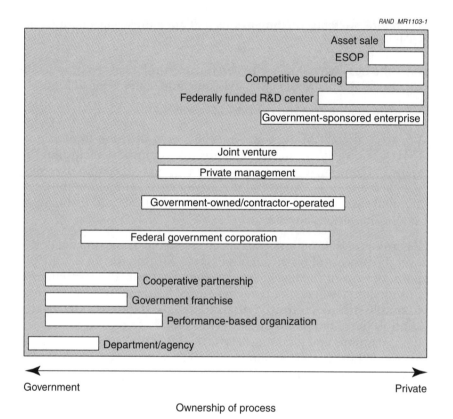

Figure 1—Alternatives Arrayed Along the Ownership of Process Dimension

The other end of the scale is anchored by asset sales. Under an asset sale, the government transfers ownership of a physical asset to another organization that is generally a private company (or perhaps a local government). The government generally relinquishes all ownership over the process in the transaction.

These same alternatives are arrayed in Figure 2 in terms of the customer/client dimension. By customers/clients, we mean who is being served by the function or activity being undertaken for the federal government: government (including other government agencies), private customers, or a mix of both.

The figure shows some interesting differences in the way that the alternatives are ranked. Clearly, government agencies serve all kinds of customers so they range across the entire spectrum. Similarly, PBOs generally serve either a mix of customers or a fully private or general public customer base. The one PBO currently extant serves the general public (students) and most of the ones proposed serve customers or clients from the general public as well. Generally, government franchises serve an internal government customer; similarly, FFRDCs and GOCOs serve government customers only and thus are not appropriate alternatives when considering activities that

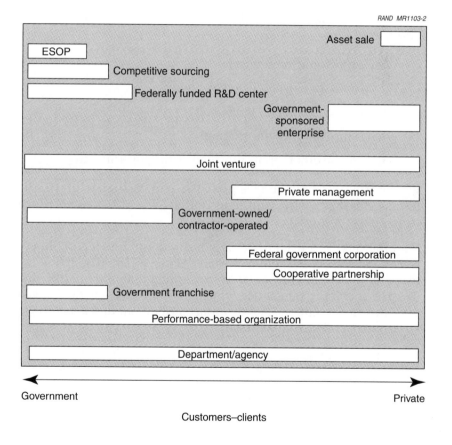

Figure 2—Alternatives Arrayed Along the Customer–Client Dimension

serve private customers or a mix of the two. The federal government corporation serves a broad spectrum of clients but seldom is created to serve a solely governmental one. Private management in the cases considered here involve the management of government facilities that serve the general public such as airports.

Obviously, other dimensions are important including the funding mechanism (direct appropriations versus contracts) and additional government inputs (i.e., assets, tax breaks). Table 1 summarizes these alternatives along a variety of dimensions that capture the important distinctions among them and should provide a useful framework for distinguishing among systems and may assist decisionmaking. The characteristics shown in the table include the following:

- Who is providing the service?

- What is the staffing of the organization?

- Who is the customer for the service?

- What is the source of the funding?

- What are the other inputs provided by the government?

We have talked about service providers and customers previously because these are fairly central to DoD's deliberation about which structure is appropriate.

Who the service provider is clearly has implications for staffing as well. With respect to staffing, the table shows a clear distinction between entities that are staffed by government employees (the first five listed) and the remainder, which are staffed by private employees. The one exception is joint ventures, where we find a mixture of government and private staffing.

In terms of funding, most receive all their funding through direct appropriations whereas a few—private management, joint ventures, and GSEs—receive their funding from direct sales. FGCs span the spectrum of funding. We distinguish between "direct appropriations" and "direct sales" because the difference has profound implications for control over a relationship and motivations for improvement. We also distinguish government assets from funds to highlight

Table 1

Options for Governance Structures/Organizational Forms

Option	Service Provider	Staff	Service Customer	Funding Mechanism	Other Govt. Inputs	Other Distinctions, Comments
Standard DoD department	Govt.	Govt.	Same govt., other govt., private	Direct appropriations (DA)	Assets	
PBO	Govt.	Govt.	Same govt., other govt., private	DA	Assets	Applies to any organization
Govt. franchise	Govt.	Govt.	Other govt.	Sales	Assets	Not DoD working capital fund, which is financed by DA
Cooperative partnership	Several govt.	Govt.	Private	DA	Assets	Mainly one-stop shopping for information
FGC	Govt., some private	Govt. or Private	Private	DA or sales	Assets, sometimes DA for deficits	Currently controls monopolies, assures uniform prices
GOCO	Govt. and private	Private	Govt.	DA	Assets	
Private management	Govt. and private	Private	Private	Sales	Assets	
Joint venture	Govt. and private	Govt. and private	Govt. and private	Sales	Assets	Rules of engagement evolving rapidly
GSE	Private	Private	Private	Sales	Loan guarantees, tax breaks	Currently focused on finance services for private customers
FFRDC	Private	Private	Govt.	DA	Assets	
Competitive sourcing	Private	Private	Govt. or private	Sales	Some assets	OMB Circular A-76 drives the process
ESOP	Private	Private	Govt.	Sales	Some assets	Can apply to any private firm; may initially receive a guaranteed contract
Asset sale	Private	Private	Govt.	Sales	Assets	Govt. gets out of the business

aThis pertains to cases in which the private contractor wins the competition. If the in-house bid wins, the provider (and staff) will still be the government.

differences in the way government agencies think about these and the difference in the way MOUs and contracts treat them.

This table provides a framework for sorting out the various alternatives in terms of several important characteristics. Given the characteristics of the activity or function being considered for reorganization or privatization, this framework can be used to delineate the proper choice set of alternative options and to limit consideration of alternatives to a smaller, more appropriate subset. The details provided in the main body of the report, along with the case studies, then will help flesh out these alternatives.

Ultimately, however, the decisionmaker needs to articulate objectives for that particular activity or function and to rank the alternatives being considered according to how well they achieve specific goals.

This introduction has provided an overview of the various alternative organizational arrangements available to the government in its efforts to remake itself into a leaner, more efficient entity. Each option shown has its own advantages and disadvantages. Thus, we should not expect a dominant or perfect policy alternative to emerge from this set of prescriptions. It is unlikely that any one alternative will be ideal, given a multiplicity of goals. It bears repeating that one should not decide on a preferred alternative until all the alternatives have been evaluated with respect to all the goals (Weimer and Vining, 1992).

Chapter Two

PERFORMANCE-BASED ORGANIZATION

Provider	Government
Staffing	Government
Customers	Government and private
Source of funding	Direct appropriations
Distinctive features	• PBO formed as a discrete management unit run by a COO
	• Policy-setting functions are retained by departmental secretary, operating functions are moved under the purview of the PBO
	• COO from outside the government provides latitude in personnel, procurement, financing, and real property
	• COO signs yearly performance contract
	• PBO must specify measurable performance goals to ensure accountability of results
Implementation issues	Requires legislation and internal support
Pros	• Performance goals are clear and understandable to all
	• Increased flexibility in personnel and acquisition
Cons	• Costs due to disruption in service delivery during the transition may be high
	• Requires a large time investment
	• Employees may object to the change
	• Unions may have concerns
Entities seeking PBO status	• Defense Commissary Agency
	• FAA Air Traffic Services Division
	• Federal Lands Highway Program
	• National Technical Information Service
	• Patent and Trademark Office
	• Rural Telephone Bank
	• Seafood Inspection Service
	• St. Lawrence Seaway Development Corporation
	• U.S. Mint
Case study	Office of Student Financial Assistance Programs

CASE STUDY: OFFICE OF STUDENT FINANCIAL ASSISTANCE PROGRAMS

Background

In a March 1996 speech to the National Press Club, Vice President Gore proposed creating PBOs within existing federal departments. Under the Higher Education Amendments of 1998, the Department of Education Student Financial Aid Program (SFAP) became the first federal PBO—the Office of Student Financial Assistance Programs (OSFAP).

A number of factors influenced the decision to turn SFAP into a PBO. Since the Clinton administration began in fiscal year 1993, student aid has rapidly expanded. Between fiscal year 1993 and fiscal year 1998, it doubled in size (Smith, 1998). Further, the diversity and number of the program's participants and the complexity of the federal aid policy and programs created performance and management concerns (Department of Education, 1997). In fact, the Advisory Committee on Student Financial Assistance had been evaluating the management and performance of the student financial aid office for over ten years. One action the committee recommended to improve the system was to restructure the management of delivery through a PBO. The Department of Education agreed to support restructuring SFAP as part of its modernization efforts (Advisory Committee on Student Financial Assistance, 1998).

Provisions of Legislation

Under Public Law 105-244, the Secretary of Education remains responsible for setting federal student aid policy and the PBO is responsible for the administration of the information and financial systems that support student financial assistance programs. The PBO is headed by a COO with demonstrated management ability and expertise in information technology. The COO reports directly to the Secretary of Education. Each year, the secretary and the COO enter an annual performance agreement that establishes measurable organizational and individual goals for the COO. The plan includes goals for service improvement, cost reduction, the improvement and integration of support systems, and the delivery system. The COO's compensation, above an established based amount, is tied to meeting the goals of the performance agreement. The PBO is given an independent operating budget and possesses increased flexibility in procurement and personnel management.

Major Facilitating Factors

The concept of creating a PBO in the Department of Education student financial aid office gained the support of education and political leadership including the Advisory Committee on Student Financial Assistance, the Education Department's Inspector General, Vice President Gore and the National Performance Review, members of Congress, and the higher education community.

Reported Results

Greg Woods was sworn in as the COO of OSFAP in December 1998. An interim performance plan is in place and the performance plan will be delivered September 1999.

Chapter Three

GOVERNMENT FRANCHISE

Provider	Government
Staffing	Primarily government, but franchise may also contract-out for services
Customers	Federal agencies and departments
Source of funding	Funding provided by fees charged to its customers; some franchises have received a direct appropriation from Congress for start-up costs
Distinctive features	Designed to operate as self-supporting, businesslike units
Implementation issues	Requires legislation
Pros	• Allows the purchasing agency to concentrate on its core mission
	• Often reduces the cost of the good/service for the purchasing agency
	• Generates revenue for the agency offering the service
Cons	• Purchasing agency risks purchasing a service that may not be delivered as promised
	• Relinquished support service capabilities may be difficult to reestablish if necessary
Examples	Department of the Treasury
	• Federal Quality Consulting Group
	• Center for Applied Financial Management
	Department of the Interior
	• Denver Administrative Support Center
	Department of Commerce
	• Office of Computer Services
	• Administrative Support Centers of the National Oceanic and Atmospheric Administration
	Department of Health and Human Services
	• Federal Occupational Health Organization
Case studies	Department of Agriculture
	• The National Finance Center
	Department of the Treasury
	• Franchise Business Activity-West (formerly a Cooperative Administrative Support Unit)

CASE STUDY: NATIONAL FINANCE CENTER

Participants

Service provider: USDA National Finance Center

Service purchaser: Federal agencies and bureaus

Background

Among federal agencies, the USDA had been the forerunner in the application of computer technology in managing administrative functions. In 1973, USDA merged its centralized payroll and personnel system and its centralized voucher and invoice processing center to form the National Finance Center (NFC). In the early 1980s, NFC developed and operated efficient and cost-effective administrative, financial, and management information systems making it a prime candidate for cross-servicing (now referred to as franchising) other federal departments and agencies. The Reagan administration encouraged cross-servicing, and in 1983, NFC began franchising its services to other federal departments and agencies (USDA National Finance Center, undated).

Today, NFC provides administrative and financial systems, including payroll, accounting, commercial vendor payments, travel, accounts receivable, and property management, to more than 120 federal agencies and bureaus. The smallest payroll/personnel customer has only two accounts and the largest has over 160,000 accounts. NFC also keeps records for the federal Thrift Savings Program that serves the entire federal community. NFC receives no direct appropriations from Congress, operating on a fee-for-service, entrepreneurial basis with its customers.

Contract Provisions

NFC establishes fee-for-service contracts with its customers. These contracts incorporate conversion and on-going operating costs.

Results

NFC is one of the largest franchising providers of administrative and financial services in the federal government. Through franchising partnerships, NFC claims to have reduced unit costs while enhancing systems and improving service quality and has saved the federal government millions of dollars. The Government Accounting Office has recognized NFC as the most experienced and successful franchising provider in the government (USDA National Finance Center, undated).

CASE STUDY: FRANCHISE BUSINESS ACTIVITY-WEST/COOPERATIVE ADMINISTRATIVE SUPPORT UNIT

Participants

Service provider: Franchise Business Activity-West

Service purchaser: Federal and municipal customers in California, Arizona, and Nevada

Background

Franchise Business Activity-West was initiated as a CASU through a pilot program in Los Angeles in 1989. The pilot's objective was to consolidate selected administrative support functions to reduce redundancy and inherent operating costs under the premise that federal agencies, at the local level, performed redundant administrative actions that could be consolidated. The program recovered all internal operating costs through a surcharge added to the products and services developed and focused on customer service and competition with existing methods and organizations in service delivery. The program was voluntary and developed according to local design and initiative (U.S. Treasury Department, undated).

Analysis showed that for the Los Angeles program to achieve cost effectiveness and profitability, the scope of delivery required expansion to geographical areas beyond the centralized federal complexes in the metropolitan Los Angeles area. The program has geographically expanded over the years to include Central and Northern California, San Diego, Nevada, Arizona, New Mexico, and Texas. The general growth of the program area is reflected in changes to the organizational designation from Los Angeles CASU in 1989 to the Southern California CASU in 1993 to the Southwest Regional CASU in 1994 (U.S. Treasury Department, undated).

In 1995, the Department of the Treasury invited Southwest Regional CASU to participate in the Franchise Fund Pilot Program that was formally approved by Congress in 1996 under the Government Management Reform Act (PL 103-356). In 1996, Southwest Regional CASU began its transition into a franchise fund. It adopted a new name, the Franchise Business Activity-West, changed its support agency from the Internal Revenue Service to the Bureau of Public Debt, and initiated a working capital fund account (U.S. Treasury Department, undated).

Contract Provisions

Franchise Business Activity-West establishes fee-for-service contracts with small, medium, and large federal and municipal agencies.

Results

Franchise Business Activity-West provides over 20 product/service packages to more than 170 federal and municipal customers. Total revenues in 1996 exceeded $9 million.

Chapter Four

COOPERATIVE PARTNERSHIP

Provider	Several governments or government agencies
Staffing	Primarily government but may include private staff, as some one-stop shops include private entities as a partner
Customers	Private
Source of funding	Direct appropriation or outside grant
Implementation issues	Requires a high level of support from all partnering agencies
Pros	• Provides more seamless, convenient services to citizens and businesses • Can stop the provision of duplicate services
Examples	• One-Stop Capital Shops • Customs and Immigration have divided the job of primary inspections for travelers entering the United States • The Department of Commerce, the Small Business Administration, and the Export-Import Bank jointly staff an Export Assistance Center to provide one-stop service to exporting businesses
Case studies	• U.S. General Store, Atlanta, Georgia • Houston U.S. General Store for Small Business

CASE STUDY: U.S. GENERAL STORE, ATLANTA, GEORGIA

Participants

Federal, state, and local government agencies and a private, non-profit organization (listed below).

Federal Executive Board (FEB), Federal Aviation Administration, Federal Communications Commission, Federal Deposit Insurance Corporation, Federal Trade Commission, Fish and Wildlife Services, Food and Drug Administration, Forest Service, General Services

Administration (GSA), Georgia Department of Labor, Georgia Department of Transportation, Goodwill Industries, Internal Revenue Service (IRS), Office of Personnel Management, National Park Service, Small Business Administration (SBA), Social Security Administration, U.S. Department of Commerce, U.S. Department of Education, U.S. Department of Energy, U.S. Department of Health and Human Services, U.S. Department of Housing and Urban Development (HUD), U.S. Department of Labor/Job Corps, U.S. Merit Systems Protection Board, U.S. Postal Service.

Description and Provisions of Agreement

The U.S. General Stores are formed through cooperative partnerships between federal, state, or local governments. The U.S. General Store in Atlanta opened in June 1996 to provide citizens with government information pertaining to federal, state, county, city, and local organizations within the community at a single location. The Federal Executive Board sponsors the store, the General Services Administration provides its manager, and the City of Atlanta donates the office space. The store opened with a contribution of $1,000 from each participating agency (Federal Benchmarking Consortium, 1997).

The store's interior resembles a bank, with counters for general services and desks for more specialized assistance. The store also contains kiosks that provide electronic information and transaction services and personal computers for Internet access. Twenty-four federal, state, and city agencies currently participate in the General Store (Federal Benchmarking Consortium, 1997).

CASE STUDY: HOUSTON U.S. GENERAL STORE FOR SMALL BUSINESS

Participants

Federal, state, and local government agencies and private sector firms (listed below).

U.S. Small Business Administration, Houston Small Business Development Corporation, Business Information Center, Internal Revenue

Service, Environmental Protection Agency (EPA), General Services Administration, SCORE-Retired Executives, City of Houston One Stop Business Center, Texas Natural Resources Conservation Commission, Department of Labor-Wage and Hour Division, Office of Federal Contract Compliance Programs, NASA, Equal Employment Opportunity Commission (EEOC), Occupational Safety and Health Administration (OSHA), U.S. Department of Housing and Urban Development, Immigration and Naturalization Service, State of Texas Comptrollers Office, U.S. Postal Service, U.S. Customs Service, Harris County DBA, Veterans Administration Medical Center, Harris County Housing and Community Development Agency, Harris County Appraisal District, Eller Media, Shell Oil, METROBANK, Academy Sports and Outdoors, Gannett Outdoor, Sykes Communications, Office of Congressman Gene Green, Office of Congressman Ken Bentsen, Office of Congresswoman Sheila Jackson Lee.

Description and Agreement Provisions

The Houston U.S. General Store for Small Business is a one-stop shop for small businesses. It provides a wide array of services such as business start-up procedures; loan information and applications; SBA loan guarantees; marketing and sales counseling; and information regarding taxes, immigration rules and regulations, and OSHA rules.

The General Store is housed in a shopping center owned by the City of Houston and is managed by a management committee that was appointed by the Houston FEB. The management committee is composed of senior managers from EEOC, SBA, GSA, HUD, and EPA. Originally, the SBA managed the store, but this proved too heavy a burden for one agency. As a result, the FEB formed the management committee. The store is staffed with two SBA employees, six Service Corps of Retired Executives (SCORE) volunteers on a rotating basis, two GSA employees, two IRS employees, a part-time City of Houston Business Center representative, a county clerk representative two afternoons per week, and an OSHA representative one-half day a week.

The store itself operates without a budget. Public and private partners have donated all services and equipment in the store including furniture, computers, workstations, and fax machines. The Houston

Small Business Development Corporation fixed the rent for the first and second year of operations at one dollar. Future financing for the store remains uncertain and is a concern.

The agencies did not execute memoranda of understanding, providing the large project flexibility in objectives, job descriptions, roles, financial participation, staffing, and training. As a substitute for memoranda of understanding, subcommittees were established to implement the program with committed agency personnel who develop strategic plans for both the short and long term (National Partnership for Reinventing Government, undated).

Facilitating Factors

The store received support from political officials. Congresswoman Sheila Jackson Lee assisted the store by providing access to the Vice President and the Mayor of the City of Houston. She also worked as an ambassador for the store's work, helping to attract customers and partners (National Partnership for Reinventing Government, undated).

The leadership and experience of the Houston Federal Executive Board also assisted in the store's success. The FEB has a history of collaboration between federal agencies and partnerships with non-governmental agencies that provided the experience needed to implement a broad collaborative effort. The FEB also had an executive director who provided strong leadership and developed an extensive communication system by fax. The communication system instantly notifies the partners and staff of important events enhancing communication among all partners (National Partnership for Reinventing Government, undated).

Chapter Five

FEDERAL GOVERNMENT CORPORATION

Provider	Government, some private
Staffing	Government or private, depending on charter
Customers	Private
Source of funding	Primarily sales; may also receive direct appropriations (e.g., Amtrak)
Distinctive features	• Operate as self-sustaining, commercial organizations (goal)
	• Provide goods and services of national importance that are not provided adequately by the private sector
	• Profit or nonprofit
Implementation issues	Legislation required
Pros	• Efficiency of execution of policy mandates from corporate and commercial structure
	• Insulation of programs from political forces
	• Off the balance sheet financing of projects
Cons	• Lack of accountability to constituencies
	• Potential conflicts with constitutional issues
Examples	• Amtrak
	• FHA
	• Eximbank
	• RTC
	• Smithsonian
	• U.S. Institute for Peace
	• National Park Foundation
	• Tennessee Valley Authority
Case studies	• U.S. Enrichment Corporation
	• U.S. Postal Service

CASE STUDY: U.S. ENRICHMENT CORPORATION

Background

With the last U.S. underground nuclear weapons test in September 1992, the demand for weapons grade enriched uranium decreased to a bare minimum. The materials production complex developed by the Department of Energy (DoE) was scaled for the fabrication of many warheads per year. With the cessation of nuclear testing, the advent of the START agreements, and the soon-to-be-signed but not ratified Comprehensive Test Ban Treaty, the utility of the materials production facilities for national security was limited. Although most of these facilities were tailored to the unique demands of nuclear weapon fabrication, the uranium enrichment plants in Portsmouth, Ohio, and Paducah, Kentucky, were already providing enrichment services to the commercial reactor industry worldwide.

These plants began providing low enriched uranium (LEU) for commercial uses in 1969 (Private Ownership of Nuclear Materials Act of 1964). During the 1970s, these plants satisfied most of the LEU needs of the Free World providing for substantial cost recovery to the U.S. government. By the 1980s, the international market was fragmenting with the emergence of several overseas competitors. When the international prices for LEU dropped and the need for weapons grade enrichment declined, the DoE was not able to recover costs as it had before.

In 1992, Congress passed the Energy Policy Act, designed to restructure the uranium enrichment program at DoE. Under the terms of this legislation, the United States Enrichment Corporation (USEC), a wholly owned government corporation, was created as the first step toward the eventual privatization of the entire DoE enrichment program. This legislation leased the two existing gaseous diffusion enrichment plants (Portsmouth and Paducah) to USEC, granted it the exclusive commercial rights to the development of the new Atomic Vapor Laser Isotope Separation (AVLIS) technology, and transferred to USEC all intellectual and property rights in this connection. The legislation also exempted USEC from many operating restrictions of the earlier form of the program.

In 1994, after its first full year of operation, USEC reported $1.4 billion in gross revenues with a net income of about $377 million. As a federal government corporation, USEC had about 88 percent of the domestic market for LEU and 40 percent of the overseas market, making it the world's largest uranium enrichment services supplier (U.S. GAO, 1995).

In 1995, a full privatization plan was submitted to the president. Two possible paths were considered: one in which USEC would be taken over in a merger or acquisition arrangement and one in which shares in USEC would be offered directly to the public in an IPO (Initial Public Offering). In either case, most of the liabilities associated with operations and the environmental issues arising from the capital leases for facilities would be retained by the government. In addition, the government would help support the recent deals with the Russian government over the transfer of many tons of high enriched uranium (HEU) from the dismantling of nuclear warheads for subsequent introduction into the international market as LEU after reprocessing. In effect, USEC became the reprocessing and sales and marketing contractor for the Russian enrichment organization, TENEX (USEC Privatization Act of 1996).

In June 1998, the IPO path was approved and USEC stock went on sale on the New York Stock Exchange (NYSE) in July of that year. Also in July of that year, $1.9 billion was transferred to the U.S. Treasury for the redemption of government ownership in USEC. The final IPO agreement contained two provisions that allowed the government and U.S. taxpayers to benefit from any windfalls in profits from the new private corporation—a claw back provision directly on profits and the issuing of warrants for USEC stock.

Major Facilitating Factors

Three major factors contributed to the success of this privatization. First, the facilities were already involved in commercial work and had established a market presence in an existing market. Second, the government was willing to structure the deal in such a way that outside investors could see an opportunity for growth with limited liability. In particular, the government assumed all liability for environmental issues and was willing to transfer all intellectual property rights for the AVLIS technology to USEC. Third, the senior leadership in the government from the White House through the department secretaries to the local managers was committed to commercializing the operation in the best possible way to extract maximal value for the government and U.S. taxpayers.

Major Constraining Factors

The side deal the government had made with the Russian government to purchase HEU from dismantled nuclear warheads and to down mix it with natural uranium so that it qualified as LEU for commercial reactor application enormously complicated the negotiations (U.S. GAO, 1995). In addition, the inability of USEC to secure favorable electrical power rates through the continuation of an existing agreement between the government and the electric power utilities made the initial operating cost estimates difficult. Subsequent arrangements before IPO resolved this difficulty.

Present Status

USEC is traded on the NYSE under the symbol USU. The largest market for the enrichment services is in Asia where recent delays in reactor refueling has caused a decline in quarterly earnings.

CASE STUDY: U.S. POSTAL SERVICE, AN INDEPENDENT ESTABLISHMENT OF THE EXECUTIVE BRANCH OF THE U.S. GOVERNMENT

Background

Even in the colonial days before the United States existed as a nation, providing for the exchange of correspondence between citizens and business concerns was considered important. Initially, Post Offices and Post Roads were supported by the British government. One of the first issues settled at the Continental Congress in 1775 was the continuation of the delivery of the mail by the colonists alone. From this early a date, the delivery of mail was considered an essential service provided by the government to its citizens that served to bind the nation together personally, politically, and economically. Although initially an organization operated as an independent agency with the Postmaster General appointed by the President, the Post

Office became a cabinet level department in 1829 during the Jackson administration.

As the country expanded during the 1800s and the early 1900s, the Post Office Department experimented with every new method of transport that became available using several new methods such as airplanes and steam ships. In many ways, the Post Office stimulated economic development as well as delivering the mail. During these times, the costs for such delivery were largely assumed by the government. The revenue recovered from postal rates was smaller than the costs of operations.

After WWII, the Post Office did not modernize as readily as it had before. Fragmented control over business processes and the workforce caused it to fall further behind private organizations conducting similar business. By the 1960s, the Post Office Department had fallen far behind in terms of management and labor practices and in terms of best industrial practice in the operations of a shipping service. It was clearly time for a change, and in 1969 the new Postmaster General in the first Nixon administration proposed to reorganize the Post Office as a wholly owned government corporation (Postal Reform Act of 1969). After lengthy hearings, Congress and the President reached a compromise, but the seven unions involved objected to the compromise provision. The unions conducted a work stoppage in March 1970 that involved most of the workforce. In response, Congress and the President agreed to create the U.S. Postal Service as a new entity, very similar to a government corporation, called an Independent Establishment of the Executive Branch of the U.S. Government (39 U.S.C. 201). The Postal Reorganization Act provided for independent control over budgets, removal of the organization from politics, collective bargaining between postal management and employees, and rate setting by the Postal Service after hearings before an impartial panel.

Major Facilitating Factors

In the 1960s, the country as a whole depended on the Post Office for delivery of personal and business correspondence. The decline in service in this decade and the evident inefficiencies prompted action. Because many of the services being delivered were of a commercial nature and because similar commercial organizations existed, templates for the new organization were clear and identifiable. A government corporation could be structured to be an instrument of both economic service and policy implementation. Policy formulation would always reside in the government itself.

Major Constraining Factors

Some of the services delivered by the Post Office are a matter of government policy and tradition and are delivered at a loss. A strictly commercial venture would simply stop the service. The new organization had to span the gap between the inherently governmental services and inherently commercial services. Many of the provisions of the legislation make these roles clear.

Present Status

The U.S. Postal Service (USPS) has substantially improved services since the 1960s with the introduction of many new technologies. Currently new modes of communication such as email and new alternative services such as United Parcel Service (UPS) or FedEx have substantially eroded the USPS market share in some niche markets. The USPS still delivers mail at a loss to some remote parts of the United States.

Chapter Six

GOVERNMENT-OWNED CONTRACTOR-OPERATED

Provider	Private and government
Staffing	Private
Customers	Government—typically a single agency
Source of funding	Government
Distinctive features	• Special target area of great importance to the government often involving hazardous materials or processes
	• Capital assets and essential government personnel can be split without disruption
	• Capital assets of unique importance to the government
	• Sometimes GOCO combined with FFRDC
Implementation issues	Standard contracting method
Pros	Commercial operation of facilities for which the government is the sole customer
Cons	Micromanagement may lead to declines in efficiency, but a lack of contract oversight can result in poor outcomes
Examples	• Air Force Plant 42
	• Sandia National Laboratory
Case studies	• Holston Army Ammunition Plant
	• U.S. Navy Military Sealift Command
	• Los Alamos National Laboratory

CASE STUDY: HOLSTON ARMY AMMUNITION PLANT

Participants

Government: Army Industrial Operations Command

Private: Eastman Chemical Company, Holston Defense Corporation subsidiary

Background

During WWI, American soldiers arrived in Europe so poorly equipped that much of the equipment needed was purchased from the French and British. Manpower could be raised far more quickly than the equipment could be manufactured. Army planners in the 1920s and 1930s committed to a plan in which the expert ability of U.S. industry at mass production would be harnessed in newly built government-owned factories that produced armaments (Kane, 1998). Because of security and safety reasons, it was felt that these facilities should be located far from the coast and in relatively remote areas. In response to the fall of Paris to Nazi troops in 1940, the first wave of construction of 29 armament facilities, operated as GOCOs, began. The Ordnance Department built the Holston Ordnance Works to Eastman Chemical specifications for the production of Composition B.

Since WWII, the Holston Works has provided munitions for the Korean Conflict, Vietnam, and Desert Storm. Now, under the Industrial Operations Command, Holston is in the process of modernizing its facilities for modern technology and new explosive formulations for the 21st century.

Holston operates on 6,000 acres of land in rural Tennessee with 425 buildings and 130 storage magazines. It employs 20 government workers, two military staff, and about 600 civilian corporate employees. The annual budget is about $60 million. In 1995, Holston was certified ISO 9002 compliant. In 1996, Holston received the Army Communities of Excellence Award.

Major Facilitating Factors

The mass production of chemical explosives was ideally suited to the expertise of the Eastman Chemical Company. With the overall GOCO contracting strategy already planned from the 1930s, the WWII national emergency rapidly marshaled U.S. industrial capacity for the war effort. The facilities for mass production of Royal Demolition Explosives (RDX) are highly specialized and not generally commercial. The processes used and the management needed are industrial. The government building of the facilities and Eastman Chemical management was an ideal match. Geographically, the availability of vast tracks of remote land in the United States made the isolation of facilities such as this possible. Finally, a government management team committed to high quality and customer service has allowed this facility to continue its contribution to national security.

Major Constraining Factors

The government invested in the facilities because it knew it would be a customer and possibly the only customer for the materials it needed. With an existing GOCO, the central issues concern excess capacity and the possible commercialization of facilities. For a new GOCO, the issues concern whether or not the government can simply contract-out for the entire service or if retaining existing facilities in this manner is a wise hedge against an uncertain future.

Present Status

Holston Army Ammunition Plant is the single active DoD producer of conventional explosives. It is the sole source supplier of high explosive powder used by DoE in the fabrication of explosive lenses used in nuclear warheads.

CASE STUDY: U.S. NAVY MILITARY SEALIFT COMMAND [1]

Participants:

Public: Department of Navy's Military Sealift Command (MSC)

Private: International Marine Carriers, Inc. (IMC)

Background

MSC is responsible for the ocean transportation of DoD supplies and equipment during both peace and war. Nine Sealift class tankers, *Sealift Atlantic, Sealift Pacific, Sealift Arabian Sea, Sealift China Sea,*

---

[1]This case draws heavily upon U.S. GAO (1994).

Sealift Indian Ocean, Sealift Mediterranean, Sealift Caribbean, Sealift Arctic, and *Sealift Antarctic,* were specifically built for, and chartered to, MSC for 20 years, 1975–1995. At the end of the charter period, MSC was obligated to return the ships to the owners in the same condition as received, less "depreciation and normal wear and tear." Although chartered to MSC, they were contractor operated and maintained. These ships provided point-to-point fuel deliveries to U.S. defense bases around the world during peacetime and were equipped to transfer fuel to other ships at sea.

The condition of the ships had begun to deteriorate under the fixed-price contract previous to the IMC contract. Internal MSC reports from November 1988 noted that under a fixed-price contract, it was not in the contractor's interest to perform up to MSC's standards and that it was difficult to make the contractor do so. Nevertheless, the next contract awarded, the IMC contract, was also fixed-price.

Upon Congressional request, the GAO conducted an investigation regarding IMC's operation of the Sealift tankers from April 1990 to May 1994.

Contract Provisions

In April 1990, MSC awarded a five-year fixed-price contract for about $170 million to IMC. The contract allowed modifications that increased MSC's payments to IMC, as of April 1, 1994, to about $256 million. The contract stipulated that the contractor was responsible for (1) providing MSC monthly reports of completed maintenance actions and keeping on board a written record of tests, inspections, and maintenance conducted; and (2) staffing a complete crew (at least 25 persons) that was qualified, had appropriate security clearances, and was of good character.

Results

A fixed-price contract needs vigilant oversight, as any funds not spent for personnel salary or maintenance remain with the contractor. However, MSC failed to provide proper oversight. MSC did not assign (1) a program manager to oversee the performance of the contract, (2) areas of responsibility and lines of authority, in writing, among various directorates involved in overseeing the contract, (3) a group with overall responsibility for the contract, and (4) initially, a Contracting Officer's Technical Representative for contract monitoring (one eventually was assigned in 1993). The lack of MSC oversight led to further deterioration of the seatankers' structure, unsafe conditions for crew, unqualified crew working the tanker, and additional costs to MSC (U.S. GAO, 1994).

IMC did not conduct preventative maintenance activities and did not submit monthly reports to MSC as required under the contract. Further, discrepancies existed between reports submitted and on-board maintenance records. Lack of maintenance resulted in lack of readiness and unsafe operating conditions. GAO found that the refueling-at-sea equipment on many tankers was frequently inoperable. Components of the equipment were frozen in place either by rust or corrosion or critical parts were missing. These deficiencies affected the ships' ability to meet their missions. During Operation Desert Storm, two tankers could not refuel at sea. MSC records also documented unsafe operating conditions on the nine tankers including excessive oil leaks; leaking fuel line and fuel pumps; inoperable lifesaving equipment including life boats; poorly maintained or inoperable fire stations; deteriorated, damaged, or missing railings on the ships' weather decks; and improperly stored chemicals and lubrication oil. Crew members on one tanker complained that a lack of gloves, boots, and respirators created health hazards when they had to clean the cargo tanks (U.S. GAO, 1994).

IMC did not meet its contractual obligation regarding crew requirements. GAO found that IMC allowed tankers to sail with a shortage of crew and that unqualified and inexperienced crew members often worked on the ships. Crew members reported high turnover because of low wages—IMC offered 10 percent less than the market rate. GAO found that over a two-year period on three ships, 658 individuals had been hired to fill the 75 crew positions—an average of over eight individuals for every position. Also, contrary to the contract, MSC did not always approve "key" crew members, including ship's master, or captain, and IMC did not forward resumes to MSC as stipulated in the contract.

Crew members' lack of qualifications and experience had serious environmental consequences. For instance, on February 4, 1991,

Sealift Caribbean spilled oil in a Houston, Texas, port. This was the ship's fourth reported spill in water since IMC's operational takeover in April 1990. It also had seven reported spills on deck during the ten-month period. Crew shortages and poorly qualified seamen were cited as the probable causes for the spills. Also, on March 1992, *Sealift Caribbean* discharged over 47,000 gallons of gasoline into the sea. Naval investigators cited the captain's "extremely poor judgement and complete ignorance of actions expected and required of him" as the reason for the discharge (U.S. GAO, 1994).

IMC did not properly screen crew members and many did not have the appropriate clearances. A GAO review of contract files showed no record of background investigations or security clearances for key crew members. MSC had not verified that the contractor had obtained appropriate clearances, and many key crew members had security clearances pending. In addition, a GAO check for criminal records of crew members who had been employed over a two-year period on the three ships GAO visited revealed that about 178 of the 658 individuals employed had been previously convicted of felonies including assault and rape; about one-third of the convictions involved various drug violations. Two individuals were fugitives. Some of the seamen had used false Social Security numbers and some were not U.S. citizens (U.S. GAO, 1994).

The lack of MSC oversight also cost MSC additional money. As a result of not enforcing the contract's maintenance requirements, MSC had to take two actions that cost MSC about $20 million. At MSC direction, the contractor hired additional crew, "wipers," to wipe up excess oil in the engine rooms and other parts of the ships. Also, beginning in August 1991, each ship underwent material upgrades costing MSC about $18 million over the original $170 million 1990 contract cost. Even after the material condition upgrade, an independent marine surveyor surveyed four tankers for the ships' owners and found serious maintenance problems. Also, MSC did not adequately inventory the government-furnished equipment and supplies left on the ships when they were turned over to IMC as the new contractor in 1990. As a result, MSC is vulnerable to IMC's claims. As of the 1994 GAO study, IMC had filed claims to recoup funds spent to purchase needed items and repair certain equipment.

To reiterate, fixed-price contracts require diligent oversight. Because of the lack of MSC oversight, IMC failed to uphold key provisions in the contract.

CASE STUDY: LOS ALAMOS NATIONAL LABORATORY

Participants

Government: Atomic Energy Commission
Energy Research and Development Agency
Department of Energy
Department of the Army
Department of Defense

Private: University of California
University of Chicago
Columbia University
Massachusetts Institute of Technology

Background

In a letter to President Roosevelt dated August 2nd, 1939, Albert Einstein urged support of efforts to develop a new and potent source of energy using the chain reaction generated by uranium. He pointed out that extremely powerful bombs could be constructed using this energy source (Groves, 1962). Although initially the possibility of such a bomb was of less interest, there was tremendous interest in the possibility of solving the long-standing problem of finding an energy source that could sustain long-duration undersea submarine missions without the need for vast quantities of oxygen (Gunn, 1939).

This appeal to Roosevelt, although very favorably received, fell into a science policy vacuum. No policy or structural mechanisms existed at the time that allowed the broader U.S. science community to advise the central government during times of national crisis. There were, however, a number of isolated and highly specialized scientific bureaus: the National Academy of Sciences, created during the Civil War; the National Research Council, created during World War I; and the Science Advisory Board of the National Academy of Sciences, created in 1933, which did not last long (largely because of the general sense that science and technology were to blame for the economic ills of the era).

Nevertheless, Roosevelt appointed his top physicist, Lyman Briggs, then head of the National Bureau of Standards, to form a committee of government experts on uranium technology. However, there were no government experts; scientific expertise in this area resided in U.S. and European universities. Meanwhile, there were further critical developments in our understanding of the chain reaction process. By the fall of 1942, it was clear to Secretary Stimson that the chain reaction would yield the release of unprecedented quantities of energy, that two isotopes of different elements could achieve this energy release, that several techniques for uranium isotope separation were possible, and that plutonium production in a reactor awaited the construction of such a device. The basic research of the past three years was about to turn into the industrial development of a weapon of war.

In September 1942, Brigadier General Leslie Groves was appointed to head what became known as the Manhattan Project. In the next year the foundations were laid for the Oak Ridge National Laboratory, the Argonne National Laboratory, and the Berkeley National Laboratory (later known at the Lawrence-Berkeley National Laboratory), and the Hanford Research Laboratory. Until 1942, very little effort had been devoted to the actual design, fabrication, and testing of the new weapon. It was generally agreed that a special laboratory was necessary for an integrated and coordinated effort. By the end of December 1942, General Groves had acquired the rights to the Los Alamos site in a remote part of New Mexico and construction of the new laboratory buildings had begun.

The organizational structure of the laboratory had Robert Oppenheimer as its scientific director and General Groves as its military commander. Initially, the plan was to have a fully military organization—a structure deemed necessary by the laboratory's military and super-secret mission. All scientists were to be commissioned officers and a cadre of civilian technical support staff was to supplement their efforts. Almost immediately, Oppenheimer ran into difficulty in recruiting scientific staff under this military organizational structure. Many felt that the differences in rank among scientists and the distance between military and civilian researchers would create friction and lower morale and that free exchange of ideas essential to the research would be inhibited by the requirements of military protocol. The military idea was a nonstarter. Oppenheimer then proposed to Groves that for the initial research phase, the organization would be civilian with a conversion to military when full-scale testing of the prototype devices began (Conant and Groves, 1943). In this initial phase, all procurement, personnel, and other operational issues would be conducted by the University of California under contract with the War Department. With Los Alamos as a civilian laboratory operated by the University of California, scientists from around the country flocked to the effort. Many accepted positions with the proviso that they would resign when the lab became a military organization. With the enormous successes of the initial and prototype testing phases, General Groves never followed up on his plan to militarize Los Alamos. To this day, Los Alamos is a civilian laboratory operated under a contract between the University of California and the Department of Energy. The government owns all the facilities and the business operations are done by contract.

The Los Alamos operational context is a GOCO but not the typical GOCO of that era. Since WWI, the Army had fostered the creation of GOCOs specifically to provide, for example, ammunition and explosives in case of war (Kane, 1998). All of the GOCOs of that era were oriented toward heavy industry and were operated by the industrial giants of the time. Even the other facilities created to support the Los Alamos weapon design effort with a supply of fissile material were heavy industry GOCOs operated by industry. Los Alamos was the first research GOCO. In keeping with its semi-academic mission, it was operated by a university. The staff that were recruited had the opportunity to work on research problems of great national importance using the most advanced and unique equipment known. The research GOCO has been the model for many other GOCOs operated by what is now the Department of Energy. These laboratories have been and continue to be at the forefront of basic and applied research in a wide variety of areas.

Major Facilitating Factors

Historical: Because Europe was at war and the United States was about to be dragged into the conflict, a sense of impending national emergency motivated academic and otherwise apolitical individuals to seek ways to contribute to the defense of their country. Moreover, there had been an enormous influx of European academics fleeing the tyranny of the Nazis. These new U.S. citizens represented the very best of European science and technology and were highly motivated to achieve the defeat of Germany and her allies.

Technical: A new understanding of the structure of matter stimulated scientists to consider the possibility of achieving a nuclear chain reaction. The neutron had only just been discovered (1932) and its existence implied a very new field of endeavor. In the mid-1930s, a German team of scientists showed that neutrons could stimulate the fissioning of uranium with the release of energy and the release of one or two neutrons. The neutrons were like a catalyst for this nuclear reaction and the extra neutrons released by the fission process could be used to catalyze subsequent fissions. A very large energy release could thus be obtained. The military applications of this possibility were evident to scientists on both sides of the Atlantic. Despite this, data vital to the effort were still published in the open literature.

Organizational: Individuals in leadership positions were willing to take the chance that a group of academics could pull off the first "big science" project in history without detailed military supervision. This set a standard of achievement that enabled future generations of leaders. Few scientists or engineers were willing to join the new research organization if it were purely military. General Groves, realizing that personnel were his most valuable asset in this project, formulated a civilian organizational structure under University of California management with an advisory military component—like a board of directors. University involvement was critical because it would set the standards of scientific and technical achievement and would structure the rewards and incentives accordingly. The military presence was critical to maintaining a focus on mission requirements. The overall structure was the first of its kind and set the foundation for science policy implementation for the next 50 years.

Major Constraining Factors

Historical: Before the creation of the Los Alamos Laboratory, no national science policy existed to allow the technical abilities of the U.S.

scientific community to be coordinated toward the achievement of an important national goal. Although the creation of the National Academy of Sciences after the Civil War and the creation of the National Research Council after WWI allowed for some coordination, there was no centralized funding for research in areas of vital need to the nation. It has often been argued that a Department of Science should be created at the cabinet level, but the scientific community has always balked at the possibility of a lack of diversity in the funding. The issue is academic freedom—a central issue to academics around the world. In the same way, during the formation of Los Alamos the research community balked at the idea that the research for the atomic bomb be done under a military organization instead of an academic one. So, just as today in many areas of government research, the central issues of that era were about personnel and not about bricks and mortar.

Technical: U.S. physicists of that era were educated basically in classical physics—Newton's laws, thermodynamics, and some atomic physics and optics. Such education was designed to facilitate their employment as physics teachers or by industry. Because there was no nationally organized source of funding for research, much of the research that was funded was directed at interesting but narrow areas of concern to U.S. industry. As a result, the United States had a cadre of physicists who knew how to do experiments in general, but whose training in nuclear physics was slim to zero. There were no experts in this new field, despite assurances to the contrary by those in industry eager to tap into the supply of defense dollars. An atmosphere of suspicion and contempt for technical opinion developed, which was conquered only by the leadership of that era.

Organizational: The military mindset of the era was to control not only the process but all the pieces and contributors to the process. In the parlance of today, it was micromanagement. Even in that era, researchers knew that there was a time to control all the details of a process and a time to let the process develop on its own. The demarcation was well known to industrial giants such as DuPont and General Electric—research finds its own way and manufacturing is tightly controlled. Because research on this scale had never before been attempted and because the research was so closely coupled to efforts in the manufacturing of the feed stock for the new weapon, it was difficult to see the important distinctions between the two arenas of effort. It took the inspired leadership of that time to make this distinction.

Present Status

The Los Alamos National Laboratory remains as one of the premier research facilities of the era. Since the operational adoption of the Comprehensive Test Ban Treaty in the first term of the current administration, the laboratory has changed enormously in its focus. Now, the focus is "stockpile stewardship" and not the development and testing of new weapons. With the loss of its former central mission, Los Alamos has struggled against misunderstanding and excessive interference on the part of Department of Energy (DoE) as it has sought to redefine its mission and importance in the national and international arenas. Indeed, recent reports have criticized DoE for its excessive government oversight and micromanagement (Task Force on Alternative Futures for the Department of Energy National Laboratories, 1995). Recent changes in leadership at the laboratory and at DoE may help in this respect.

Chapter Seven

PRIVATE MANAGEMENT

Provider	Private and government
Staffing	Private
Customers	Private
Source of funding	Sales or direct appropriations depending upon agreement; industry may also provide an investment
Distinctive features	Commercial operation of government-owned capital assets to provide a service to the public
Implementation issues	• Standard contracting method
	• Legislation may be required
Pros	• Provides commercial operation of public facility
	• Alternative to public financing of facility in case of sales-based financing
Cons	• Services may not be delivered as promised
Examples	• Indianapolis Airport
	• Atlantic City Airport
	• Albany Airport
Case studies	Private management of airports

CASE STUDY: PRIVATE MANAGEMENT OF AIRPORTS

Participants

Government: Municipal and county governments
Federal Aviation Agency (FAA)

Private: British Airport Authorities, Inc.
Domestic and International Airlines

Background

In 1978, the government deregulated airline ticket prices but re-tained ownership of the air traffic control system and control over the airports through the provisions of the government grants that had been used in their construction (Airline Deregulation Act of 1978). Under deregulation and generally positive economic factors, the use of U.S. airlines and airports enormously expanded. Now, 20 years later, the remaining government-owned assets in the air trans-port industry are under pressure to modernize and accommodate a still rapidly expanding industry. The government ownership and management of airports and the air traffic control system are these remaining assets. Whereas market forces have driven the expansion of the airline industry after deregulation, government ownership and management have inhibited a similarly market-driven expansion of airport services and the air traffic control system.

The privatization of airports was internationally led by Margaret Thatcher when she privatized the British Airport Authority (BAA) in 1987. It had become clear in Britain that the British airport system was very inefficient and very expensive to operate. It also was found that this system had great potential for revenue growth and efficiency gains if the old business model of operating as a traditional public utility was forsaken in favor of a new commercial model for airport management. In the British model, both the ownership and management of the airports were turned over to BAA Inc., a publicly traded corporation.

With the success in Britain of the BAA, federal, state, and local opera-tors of airports in the United States studied the possibility of a similar approach here. All public airports in the United States were devel-oped using grant funds from the FAA as well as funds from local community bond issues and direct investment by the airline com-panies. The FAA grant funds contain significant restrictions on the use of any revenues from airport operations that inhibit the com-mercialization of many airport areas. In particular, any net revenues must be used to better the airport facility (U.S. GAO, 1996).

Because the direct sale of airport assets as well as any form of a lease arrangement was very problematic, many communities sought a pri-vate management arrangement for the government-owned airport facility (U.S. GAO, 1996). In many ways, U.S. airports are already staffed by subcontractors. According to a GAO survey, only 10 percent of people working at 69 of the largest airports are public employees (U.S. GAO, 1996). Under the private management arrangement, the general contractor would be private as well.

The first airport in the United States to be operated under private management was the Indianapolis Airport in 1995. The management contract was won by British Airport Authority, US, Inc.

Major Facilitating Factors

The dramatic increase in air traffic and the increasingly important role an airport plays in a local economy emphasized to local communities the importance of efficient and well-run airports. Moreover, the need for significant expansion of many airport facilities required a financial alternative to the conventional issue of a bond in many localities. These economic reasons are the main drivers for commercialization of U.S. airports.

Major Constraining Factors

The initial financing for all airports in the United States came from the government through an FAA grant. These facilities are limited in what can be done with excess revenues, thus inhibiting any incentives for commercialization.

Current Status

Currently, airports overseas are rapidly privatizing, whereas in the United States privatization has been more cautiously approached.

Chapter Eight

PUBLIC/PRIVATE PARTNERSHIP OR JOINT VENTURE

Provider	Private and government
Staffing	Private and government
Customers	Private and government
Source of funding	Sales
Distinctive features	Often involves the renovation, construction, operation, maintenance, or management of a facility or system
Implementation issues	• May require legislation
	• Contract
	• Business plan
	• Stakeholder support
Pros	• Creates effective management of properties
	• May prove lucrative to public and private entities
	• Accesses private funds and expertise not available in an agency
	• Takes less time than disposing property under GSA regulations
Cons	• Members of agency may resist change
	• New organizational structures within an agency may be needed
Examples	• Norfolk Port Facilities
	• Soldier Housing at Fort Drum
	• Thayer Hotel, West Point
Case studies	• Fort Mason Project
	• Rincon Center
	• Houston Regional Office Center Project
	• Cold Spring Medical Facility

CASE STUDY: THE FORT MASON PROJECT[1]

Participants

Public: The Golden Gate National Recreation Area (GGNRA) in California, managed by the Department of Interior's National Park Service

Private: The Fort Mason Foundation, a private, nonprofit organization

Background

The lower Fort Mason area, located in San Francisco, is a historically significant site, as it was a major point of embarkation for American troops bound for the Pacific Theater during WWII. In 1973, the U.S. Army transferred responsibility for its maintenance, restoration, and use to GGNRA. In 1975, a Park Service study determined that the unoccupied structures of the lower Fort Mason area were subject to vandalism and deterioration. The GGNRA lacked the funds and expertise to restore and develop the lower Fort Mason facilities to the standard required by the Historic Preservation Act of 1966.

Also during this period, nonprofit groups expressed an interest in moving to the area, which is near the heart of central San Francisco. The Park Service held a series of meetings with those groups. In 1976, business and civic leaders created the Fort Mason Foundation to negotiate with the Park Service on behalf of the nonprofit community. In 1977, the foundation provided a plan to administer the warehouses and piers as a low-cost public use space and to assist nonprofit organizations in their efforts to provide cultural, educational, and recreational activities to the public.

Public/Private Cooperation Provisions

Under the cooperative agreement, the Park Service provides the buildings rent free. In return, the foundation is required to (1) renovate, maintain, and operate the lower Fort Mason area and (2) de-

---

[1]This case draws heavily upon U.S. GAO (1999b).

velop and administer the Fort Mason Center to provide cultural, recreational, and educational programs to the public at minimum or no cost. The center provides low-cost leases at rates approved by the Park Service to nonprofit groups and other outside parties. The original 1976 agreement expired in 1984 and was replaced by another agreement that expires in 2004.

Major Facilitating Factors

Three primary factors facilitated the partnership between GGNRA and the foundation. First, GGNRA was financially unable to maintain the Fort Mason buildings. The partnership provided a way for the Park Service to address the problems without increasing funding or staffing at GGNRA. Second, local residents supported the creation of a nonprofit center to avoid overcommercialization of the site and created the foundation. Park officials noted that negotiating with a strong, unified organization was key to implementing the partnership. Third, the general superintendent of GGNRA provided dynamic leadership and was willing to innovate and take risks (U.S. GAO, 1999b).

Major Constraining Factors

The newly formed Fort Mason Foundation had no track record in this business. However, this constraint was somewhat mitigated by the experience and expertise of those chosen to serve on the foundation's board of directors (U.S. GAO, 1999b).

Reported Results

The historic character of the lower Fort Mason area is preserved. The nine buildings and two piers constituting the complex have been fully renovated and maintained over the past 22 years at minimal cost to the Park Service. Further, the partnership meets one of the Park Service's and foundation's objectives—to assist nonprofit organizations in their efforts to provide activities at little to no charge to the public. The foundation leases space at low cost, about $8 per square foot, which is about 60–70 percent less than current rental market prices, to 50 residential nonprofit organizations.

CASE STUDY: THE RINCON CENTER PROJECT[2]

Participants

Public: The U.S. Postal Service

Private: Rincon Center Associates (RCA)

Background

In 1979, the Postal Service announced its intention to vacate and sell the Rincon Annex 3.5 acre postal facility, located in the "South of Market" area of San Francisco, as the operation of the facility had become inefficient. After the announcement, the Postal Service decided to consider developing the site instead. In 1985, the Postal Service issued a request for proposal (RFP) for the renovation of the existing buildings plus construction of new space. The RFP required that all competitors submit bids that included plans for (1) a central atrium or shopping core, (2) the division of the new construction into two buildings or towers, (3) compliance with historic preservation requirements, and (4) provisions for affordable housing. The Postal Service selected RCA from the seven submitted proposals.

Public/Private Cooperation Provisions

The partnership between the Postal Service and RCA was a lease/develop/operate arrangement. The property was developed by RCA subject to a 65-year ground lease of the air rights from the Postal Service. Under the lease, RCA agreed to (1) build structures above and around the original Rincon Annex building including 240,000 square feet of commercial space and two towers containing 260,000 square feet of residential space constructed over the commercial base, (2) renovate the existing Rincon Annex building into office and retail space, (3) build a 72,000-square-foot rooftop addition to the annex, (4) preserve the exterior of the original Rincon Annex and the historic murals within, (5) operate and maintain all the properties on the site, and (6) set aside a portion of the housing units for use by

---

[2]This case draws heavily upon U.S. GAO (1999b).

low- to moderate-income families. At the end of the 65-year lease, the building reverts to Postal Service ownership.

Major Facilitating Factor

The Postal Reorganization Act of 1970 directed the Postal Service to operate in a businesslike manner and authorizes the Postal Service to manage its properties using businesslike arrangements.

Major Constraining Factor

RCA and the Postal Service faced constraints in their construction options and their agreement process because of local requirements for low- and moderate-income housing and the need to fulfill the city's architectural requirements while preserving its historic character (U.S. GAO, 1999b).

Reported Results

The historical characteristics of both the original Rincon Annex post office and the murals have been preserved and currently the Postal Service receives about $4.5 million per year in ground rent. This amount has increased about 60 percent from the start of the lease. The property is leased at 100 percent, but because of cost overruns during construction and a soft real estate leasing market during Rincon Center's first several years of operations, RCA reports that the property has been only moderately successful.

In December 1998, Postal Service officials reported that they are in the process of selling the bulk of the Rincon Project to the private developer.

CASE STUDY: THE HOUSTON REGIONAL OFFICE CENTER PROJECT[3]

Participants

Public: Department of Veterans Affairs (VA)

Private: Amelang Partners, Inc. (API), a private sector real estate developer

Background

In 1992, VA's 20-year lease with the General Services Administration for the VA Houston Regional Office was about to expire. VA believed that the building was in serious disrepair and chose to relocate the regional office to the grounds of the VA Medical Center (VAMC) campus that had approximately 20 acres of available land. By moving, VA could reduce costs and enhance service to veterans by placing the office near other campus services.

In 1992, Congress provided VA with $17 million to build the new Houston Regional Office on the VAMC campus. VA officials chose to use an enhanced-use lease (EUL) agreement instead of designing and building the facility in house. Under an EUL, VA can lease VA-controlled property to the private sector or private entities for long-term use for non-VA uses in exchange for receiving fair consideration, monetary or in-kind, that enhances VA's mission or programs. VA sponsored a national competition to develop the site for a regional office building and some VA-approved commercial developments. Eight developers submitted proposals to develop the site. In January 1993, VA selected API to develop the property.

Enhanced-Use Lease Provisions

Under the 35-year EUL, API agreed to design, build, and maintain the Houston VA Regional Office building, add 500 parking spaces, and develop and maintain the remainder of the 20-acre site with commercial buildings. API owns and operates 29,000 square feet of

---

[3]This case draws heavily upon U.S. GAO (1999b).

commercial property and provides VA with a percentage of the rents. VA and the City of Houston first approve all private development proposed for the site. API assumed all financial obligations and risks associated with private development. In return for providing API with commercial development rights, VA obtained long-term operation and maintenance services at reduced costs.

The EUL also contained an agreement that VA would lease-purchase the regional office building within a one-year period after its construction. At the end of the 35-year lease, VA will own the commercial properties API developed and now leases.

Major Facilitating Factors

The primary facilitating factor for the project was the 1991 legislation authorizing EULs, as it enabled VA to keep lease payments from EUL projects and use them to fund appropriate VA activities. Also, the EUL program eliminated or streamlined many processes required in government acquisitions. For example, VA did not have to adhere to federal contracting procedures (U.S. GAO, 1999b).

Reported Results

After 11 months of construction, in March 1995, the building and parking facility were completed. As of September 1998, all commercial development was completed and all businesses were open. API currently pays VA about $75,000 annually from revenues of the commercial development. This amount is in addition to the one-time $75,000 rental payment made by the developer at the execution of the lease.

VA reports that the EUL reduced the time needed to structure and execute the development and resulted in significant cost savings over VA's design and development of the property by itself. In May 1995, this project earned a Hammer Award from Vice President Gore's National Performance Review (U.S. GAO, 1999b).

CASE STUDY: THE COLD SPRING MEDICAL FACILITY PROJECT[4]

Participants

Public: Department of Veterans Affairs

Private: State of Indiana

Background

In 1932, the federal government built the Cold Spring VA Medical Center on 30 acres in Indianapolis, Indiana. In 1950, VA opened a new hospital facility approximately 1.5 miles from Cold Spring and converted the Cold Spring facility into a veterans' psychiatric facility. In 1995, VA decided to close Cold Spring because of the declining number of patients using the facilities and a trend from inpatient to outpatient care. Under traditional federal property management and disposal procedures, VA faced either maintaining the Cold Spring facility or undertaking a disposal process through the General Services Administration that could take three to four years to complete. Instead, under EUL authority, VA entered negotiations with Indiana in January 1996. In September 1996, VA signed an EUL with Indiana leasing 22.29 acres of the 30-acre Cold Spring facility.

Enhanced-Use Lease Provisions

VA signed an EUL with Indiana. Under an EUL, VA can lease VA-controlled property to the private sector or private entities for long-term use for non-VA uses in exchange for receiving fair consideration, monetary or in-kind, that enhances VA's mission or programs. In this case, the EUL established a 35-year lease of the Cold Spring Medical Facility to the state in return for a one-time direct payment of $200,000 to VA and a payment of $9.8 million that was placed in a VA EUL trust. Under the trust agreement, VA is to use these funds to provide benefits for veterans residing in Indiana. However, the Secretary of Veterans Affairs may designate the Provision of Veterans' benefits without regard to residency.

---

[4]This case draws heavily upon U.S. GAO (1999b).

Major Facilitating Factors

The 1991 legislation authorizing EULs facilitated this agreement, as it enabled VA to keep lease payments from EUL projects and use them to fund appropriate VA activities. Also contributing to the venture's success was the fact that Indiana needed an updated mental hospital but did not have the money to refurbish their old hospital or build a new one (U.S. GAO, 1999b).

Major Constraining Factors

The venture was constrained by a few factors. First, VA regional and headquarters officials were initially concerned because the partnership differs from the traditional way the federal government manages and disposes of excess property. Second, VA met opposition from the Cold Spring medical personnel who did not want to move out of the Cold Spring facility. Third, VA officials reported concerns regarding the timetable for Congressional review set by EUL legislation. Under EUL legislation, final action cannot be taken on a proposed partnership for a period of 60 days during which Congress must be in session to allow Congress sufficient time to review and comment on the proposal. VA staff reported that the EUL private sector partners sometimes grow impatient with this requirement, as it slows down the approval process up to several months, depending on the Congressional calendar (U.S. GAO, 1999b).

Reported Results

Indiana provided VA with both monetary and in-kind considerations with an estimated total of $15.64 million. In addition, VA expects to realize annual savings of $5 million by avoiding recurring maintenance and operating costs, and Indiana saved between $10 and $15 million in significant renovation or construction of a new facility.

The project received a Hammer Award from the Vice President's National Performance Review.

Chapter Nine

GOVERNMENT-SPONSORED ENTERPRISE

Provider	Private
Staffing	Private
Customers	Private
Source of funding	Sales
Distinctive features	• Implicit guarantees of performance by the government provide favorable loan conditions for the GSE
	• Some GSEs exempted from state and local taxes
	• No immunity privileges from tort claims
	• Not subject to governmental due process restrictions
	• Not subject to Securities and Exchange Commission (SEC) regulations
Implementation issues	Legislation required
Pros	Stimulate economic growth for specific economic groups through credit availability in the private sector
Cons	Due to federal sponsorship, GSEs pose potential risks and costs to taxpayers, as the government is potentially liable for a GSE's obligations
Examples	• Farm Credit System
	• Federal Home Loan Bank System
	• Farmer Mae
	• Freddie Mac
Case studies	Fannie Mae

CASE STUDY: FANNIE MAE

Background

Congress created the Federal National Mortgage Association (Fannie Mae) in 1938 to stimulate economic growth in the housing industry by making home loans available to low- and middle-income citizens. Originally chartered as a government corporation wholly owned and controlled by the Federal Housing Authority, Fannie Mae was fully privatized in 1968 with stock trading on the NYSE. Currently, Fannie Mae is the third largest corporation in the United States in terms of assets and operates under a Congressional charter. Five members of its board of directors are appointed by the President. Fannie Mae does not make loans directly to consumers. It operates in the secondary loan market by buying loans already set up by private banks. Because of its Congressional charter, it focuses on buying loans of low- and middle-income individuals. By creating a secondary market for loans to these individuals, Fannie Mae encourages private banks to execute such loans and thus fulfills its charter.

Fannie Mae benefits from the perception by the market of the implicit support of the government in the event of default on its debt obligations. Because of this, Fannie Mae can borrow money at lower rates than comparable private organizations. The savings in rates are passed on in part to the original home buyers as well as to the owners of Fannie Mae stock.

Major Facilitating Factors

At the end of the Great Depression, the housing market and the banking institutions were still lagging in recovery. The Roosevelt administration incentivized economic growth in these markets by creating a secondary market for low-income home loans by chartering Fannie Mae. Because of the longevity of loans (10–30 years), the administration wanted to set up an organization that would not only be efficient in providing the economic stimulus but also be insulated from the vagaries of changes in political landscape. Fannie Mae leverages the perceived support of the government to obtain low rates on its debt obligations, and it passes these savings on to the home borrowers and to its stockholders.

Present Status

Fannie Mae is the third largest publicly traded corporation in the United States and still fulfills its charter to supply home loans to low- and middle-income families.

Chapter Ten

FEDERALLY FUNDED RESEARCH AND DEVELOPMENT CENTER

Provider	Private
Staffing	Private
Customers	Government
Source of funding	Direct appropriations
Distinctive features	For research and development only
Implementation issues	Legislation
Pros	• Objective research and analysis
	• Insulation from political pressures
	• Flexibility in staffing and acquisition
	• Establishes long-term relationships between the FFRDC and the sponsor allowing the FFRDC to conduct long-term research
Cons	• Loss of mission focus
	• Requires extended Congressional support
	• Competition with private industry
Examples	• Arroyo Center
	• Project Air Force
	• Center for Naval Analyses
	• IDA
Case studies	• National Defense Research Institute
	• Aerospace
	• Jet Propulsion Laboratory

CASE STUDY: NATIONAL DEFENSE RESEARCH INSTITUTE

Participants

Public: DoD, Office of the Secretary of Defense (OSD)

Private: RAND

Background

The National Defense Research Institute (NDRI) is an FFRDC within RAND that provides studies and analyses to policymakers in the Office of the Secretary of Defense, the Joint Staff, the Unified Commands, the defense agencies, and other sponsors. NDRI brings together science, analytical rigor, and an understanding of world and national security affairs to the study and choice of policy.

NDRI operates through three centers whose research corresponds closely with the responsibilities of three of the undersecretaries in the Office of the Secretary of Defense—Policy, Acquisition and Technology, and Personnel and Readiness—who are the principal sponsors of NDRI research. NDRI's centers support sponsors in a number of ways—framing new policies; defining and suggesting how to implement current policies; and studying complex problems where multidisciplinary capability, objectivity, independence, and an explicit national-interest charter are essential. At the same time, sponsors turn to NDRI to provide analytic and technical support informed by the results of its long-term research.

Major Facilitating Factors

The availability of highly skilled and knowledgeable analysts at RAND was the major facilitating factor in establishing this FFRDC.

Major Constraining Factors

The budgets for FFRDCs are capped in the enabling appropriation and authorization legislation each year.

Present Status

NDRI continues to contribute to the policy analysis requirements of OSD.

CASE STUDY: AEROSPACE

Participants

Public: DoD, Department of the Air Force

Private: Aerospace Corporation, El Segundo, California

Background

The launch of Sputnik in October 1957 refocused the attention of the United States on technological leadership and in particular on technological hegemony in space. After many booster failures, the United States put a small satellite into orbit in 1958. In that same year, legislation created the National Aeronautics and Space Administration (NASA) as a civilian organization and specifically partitioned all space activities related to national security as separate and distinct under the supervision and control of DoD (Public Law 85-568). The importance of space as a location for national security assets was of high priority at DoD. The need for outstanding world class research as well as world class mastery of launch operations was apparent from the frequent launch and mission failures of that era. These needs and the record of success at the other FFRDCs prompted the Secretary of the Air Force to create the Aerospace Corporation as the home for the new FFRDC.

Aerospace is responsible for all aspects of space system architecture as well as launch system readiness for all national security space-related activities. Their primary customers are the Space and Missile Systems Center (SMC) of the Air Force Materiel Command and the National Reconnaissance Office (NRO). Aerospace also supports the space activities of other government agencies and international organizations when it is in the national interest.

The primary mission of Aerospace is to ensure the mission success of national security space programs. Thus, Aerospace is involved in every phase of space systems development from concept and design through deployment and operations. The FFRDC structure offers the technical expertise and organizational continuity to manage space systems that typically have lifetimes of a decade or more.

Major Facilitating Factors

With the partitioning of civilian space and military space provided for by the National Aeronautics and Space Act, DoD needed to create a counterpart to NASA to focus on the national security aspects of space systems and launch vehicles.

Major Constraining Factors

Staffing was the biggest limitation in the early days of the space program. The scramble in the late 1950s and early 1960s to get the United States into space in response to the Sputnik launch created a huge demand for technical specialists in a wide variety of areas. With NASA, Aerospace, and a large number of commercial contractors actively recruiting technical specialists, the supply of skilled workers was exhausted. For a time, the educational system in the United States was not turning out enough technically oriented students at all grade levels to fulfill the expected demand.

Present Status

Aerospace Corporation currently employs 3,000 staff members. In the past decade of operation, Aerospace-supported satellite systems have had only one failure out of 85 successes.

CASE STUDY: JET PROPULSION LABORATORY

Participants

Public: National Aeronautics and Space Administration

Private: California Institute of Technology, Pasadena, California

Background

The Jet Propulsion Laboratory (JPL) grew out of the staff and facilities of the Guggenheim Aeronautical Laboratory at the California Institute of Technology. In the early 1930s, this laboratory was involved in the development of liquid and solid rockets. The initial government funding came from the Army Air Corps to develop Jet Assisted Take Off Rockets. During WWII, these rockets were commercially produced to JPL specifications. With the advent of V1 and V2 rockets by the Germans, JPL became active in the development of a U.S. version of such a device. JPL pioneered telecommunication by means of devices launched by a rocket and the ground control facilities needed to support launch activities. By the time of Sputnik in October 1957, many of the ingredients for a U.S. response were already available at JPL. Explorer I was launched in January 1958. With the creation of NASA in that same year, JPL was transferred from the Army to NASA.

By the 1960s, JPL became involved in the remote exploration of the solar system using robotic probes and less involved in the development of rockets or jet propulsion. The Ranger and Surveyor probes of the Moon supported the Apollo program with advanced information about lunar surface features and landing sites. Every satellite launched for the exploration of the solar system was designed and operated by JPL.

Major Facilitating Factors

The existence of a university laboratory conducting research in exactly the area that was needed by the Army Air Corps before WWII was a fortuitous circumstance. For NASA, the existence of a laboratory involved in the technologies and equipment needed to respond to Sputnik was also fortuitous.

Major Constraining Factors

The advent of the Space Shuttle Program in the early 1970s and NASA reliance on the shuttle as the sole satellite launch vehicle for the 1970s and beyond reduced the number of launch vehicles available for satellite deployment. By the time the commercial market for communications satellites had matured, the United States had very limited capability in this area. For all JPL missions, the shuttle had been mandated. This reduced the opportunities for alternative launch systems.

Present Status

Today, JPL serves as the principal NASA center for solar system exploration.

Chapter Eleven

COMPETITIVE SOURCING

Provider	Private
Staffing	Private
Customers	Government
Source of funding	Direct appropriation
Distinctive features	OMB Circular A-76 requirements drive the process for many types of competitive sourcing; depots are specifically excluded from A-76 requirements
Implementation issues	• Standard contracting methods; sometimes requires A-76 study
	• Legislation required for certain services
Pros	• Allows agency or organization to concentrate on core competencies
	• Contracting-out may provide a lower-cost, higher-quality product than in-house provision
	• If an organization truly thinks about the desired product/service, contracting-out may provide the government greater control over the service/product
Cons	• Without proper contract oversight, fraud, waste, and abuse can occur
	• Initial savings estimates can be overstated
	• Employee and union resistance
	• Services may not be delivered as promised
	• Relinquished capabilities may be difficult to reestablish, if desired
Case studies	• A-76 competition, Altus Air Force Base, Oklahoma
	• A-76 competition, Parris Island, South Carolina
	• Aircraft and Missile Guidance System Depot Repair
	• Single Contracts for Multiple Support Services
	• Navy Aviation Maintenance Contract, TA-4J Skyhawks
	• The U.K. Inland Revenue Service
	• The British Army Logistics Information Systems Agency

CASE STUDY: A-76 COMPETITION, ALTUS AIR FORCE BASE, OKLAHOMA

Participants

Public: Air Force

Private: Most Efficient Organization (MEO) (in-house)

Background

In October 1994, the Air Force initiated a large A-76 competition for all aircraft maintenance at Altus Air Force Base (AFB), Oklahoma. Altus AFB is the U.S. Air Force's only Strategic Airlift and Air Refueling Training Center. Its primary mission is to provide quality training to produce combat-ready aircrew members for the Air Force. Aircraft maintenance at Altus currently includes full maintenance and support of all C-5, KC-135, C-141 transient aircraft, engine, and associated ground equipment, and C-17 backshop support.

The competition included 1,401 military positions and 43 civilian positions. Five contractors submitted proposals to compete against the MEO. After a six-month period of study of the submitted proposals, it was announced that the MEO won the competition. The in-house win required that the Air Force convert a workforce of 1,444 military personnel and 43 civilian personnel to a workforce of 742 civilians. The MEO was awarded a $165.5 million multiyear award that is expected to save $99.6 million over the life of the contract. The Altus contract is the largest contract to oversee all aircraft maintenance that the Air Education and Training Command has ever awarded to an in-house organization (U.S. GAO, 1999a).

The entire effort took 23 months, 17 of which involved some contracting actions. The A-76 study took place concurrently with roughly one-half of the entire procurement process (U.S. GAO, 1997b).

Results

According to Air Force officials, problems have been associated with the transition of the workload at Altus. Specifically, full implementation of the MEO had to be extended 17 months—from December 1996 to April 1998—because of hiring problems. The winning competition required transitioning from a mostly military operation to one operated by government civilians. As a result, heavy civilian recruiting was necessary to get the MEO running. Altus found that it needed time to recruit enough personnel for the work. During the transition, the Air Force arranged for some of the maintenance work to be completed by other organizations. During the transition, the Air Force consolidated its personnel function into one location, causing further delays in hiring (U.S. GAO, 1999a).

No cost comparison data are available yet.

CASE STUDY: A-76 COMPETITION: BASE OPERATING SUPPORT AT PARRIS ISLAND, SOUTH CAROLINA[1]

Participants

Public: Marine Corps

Private: Contractor

Background

Parris Island, a Marine Corps Training Depot (MCTD), is one of the two Marine Corps boot camps. All male recruits from east of the Mississippi and all female recruits attend boot camp at Parris Island. MCTD-Parris Island also houses specialized schools such as Noncommissioned Officer (NCO) Leadership, Field Music, and Personnel Administration. In 1982, MCTD-Parris Island began an A-76 study for a multifunction base operating support (BOS) contract that included refuse collection/disposal, grounds and surface maintenance, family housing, and other building maintenance.

The A-76 competition that lasted five years was won by a contractor headquartered in North Carolina that bid $19 million. The MEO bid was $27 million. Officials used a two-step sealed-bid process in which the lowest bid wins. The contract was a small business set-

---

[1]Case material comes from Tighe et al. (1997).

aside. Only three small businesses bid on the contract and no local company bid. The fixed-price contract that included an indefinite quantity/delivery portion ran for one base year plus four option years. This contract displaced 263 government workers. Of these individuals, 12 percent retired, 31 percent were reassigned, and 57 percent were separated. According to Parris Island personnel, on the contract start date, 217 of the 263 displaced workers had jobs. A year passed between the contract win and the contract start date in 1988.

Results

The Paris Island BOS contract had many problems and resulted in the work being brought back in house in 1992.

When the contractor took over BOS services in 1988, a worse situation than expected existed. The long A-76 process had reduced morale, especially during the one-year period between the contract award and contract start. The most qualified workers left quickly and those who remained were not as productive. As a result, serious backlogs accumulated.

Great tension existed between MCTD-Parris Island managers and the contractor. Quality assurance (QA) evaluators monitored the contractor's performance and required that substandard work be redone. Many conflicts and performance arbitration proceedings between the contractor and the QA inspectors occurred. A large proportion of the disputes concerned government-furnished equipment and supplies such as the steam-generating power plant and the sewage treatment plant. The government argued that they were not being properly maintained and operated whereas the contractor demanded improvements and upgrades to the facilities.

Further, MCTD-Parris Island managers found that the indefinite quantity delivery (IDQ) component of the contract was too small to respond to surge requirements. The contract had capped the IDQ jobload at average levels. As a result, "above average" requirements had to be negotiated as a change order with the contractor.

In 1991, the contractor filed for bankruptcy for reasons unrelated to the Parris Island contract. As a result, MCTD-Parris Island chose to bid the contract again and selected a new contractor from eight bidding firms. In this contract, the performance work statement was more complete and the new contract featured more penalties for nonperformance. The contract was for $44 million over a five-year period—substantially more than the initial MEO bid of $31 million (1991 dollars).

In 1992, only ten months into the contract, the government declared that the contractor had defaulted and chose to bring the functions back in house. When the second contractor defaulted, workers were offered the chance to stay on and transition to the in-house workforce. Of more than 200 employees, roughly 160 stayed on as temporary government employees. Eventually, 130 became full-time government workers.

Lessons Learned

Tighe et al. (1997) report lessons learned from the Parris Island experience. First, there is a learning curve on both sides when outsourcing and recent outsourcing initiatives by Parris Island have been successful. Second, the long competition process is extremely difficult for morale and may affect work performance and the condition of the workload the contractor is assuming. Thus, competitions should be performed as quickly as possible and long delays between the contract award date and contract start date should be avoided.

Tighe et al. also suggest that when contracting for a service where accountability is easily blurred, such as contractor operation of in-house power plant, an arm's-length relationship may not work well. They also note that a negotiated competitive process rather than a sealed-bid process would have better protected quality. Further, industry standards and practices should play a key role in designing performance work statements and performance-based contracts.

CASE STUDY: AIRCRAFT AND MISSILE GUIDANCE SYSTEM DEPOT REPAIR[2]

Participants

Public: U.S. Air Force

Private: Boeing North American, Inc., and Wyle Laboratories

Background

Aerospace Guidance and Metrology Center (AGMC) was closed as a result of a decision of the Base Realignment and Closure Commission (BRAC). BRAC recommended the closure of AGMC, noting that the workload could be privatized or moved to other depot maintenance sites. Before closure, AGMC supported depot maintenance and metrology and calibration.

In response to the BRAC recommendation, the Air Force moved a small portion of AGMC's Air Force workload to other Air Force depots, the Navy moved most of its AGMC workload to other sites, and the Army moved all of its workload to other sites. The Air Force decided to privatize-in-place the remaining AGMC workloads. At the time of this decision, the Air Force relied on an analysis that estimated that privatizing would save about $5 million in 1997. Since October 1996, the Newark, Ohio, facility has been operated as the Boeing Guidance Repair Center (BGRC) by two contractors—Boeing North American, Inc. (Autonetics Electronics Systems Division) and Wyle Laboratories.

After a nine-month transition period, the first full year of the BGRC contract operations began in October 1996. After the first quarter, Ogden and Oklahoma City logistics center personnel noted that funds were being expended faster than anticipated for the BGRC contract. As a result, Headquarters, Air Force Materiel Command (AFMC) undertook an evaluation that compared contractor versus Air Force depot costs for the FY 1997 workload. The analysis compared both actual and estimated aircraft and missile inertial navigation system repair and metrology costs at the Boeing Guidance

---

[2]This case draws heavily upon U.S. GAO (1997b).

Repair Center to actual historic costs for comparable workloads prior to privatization-in-place.

Contract Provisions

In December 1995, the Air Force awarded Rockwell International a five-year $246 million cost-plus-award-fee contract to assume AGMC's repair mission and awarded a five-year $19 million cost-plus-award-fee contract to Wyle Laboratories to operate the metrology laboratory. In 1996, Boeing acquired Rockwell International and assumed Rockwell's contract. The Air Force retained about 130 government employees at Newark to review and certify the operations of the Air Force's 130 metrology laboratories and to assist the Defense Contract Management Command in monitoring Wyle Laboratories' metrology contract.

Reported Results of Interim Study

An Air Force interim evaluation found that the first full year of operations at the privatized-in-place center will likely cost $14.1 million more (a 16 percent cost increase) than it would have cost if the facility had continued to operate as a public activity.[3] Estimates ranged from a $7.7 million to a $31.2 million increase. The study identified three cost factors that contributed to increased costs at the facility: material costs, contract administration, and award fees. The Air Force study estimated an increased material cost of $3.4 million. Although there has been increased ordering of material, it is uncertain how material consumption will compare over a longer period. Considering the significant increase in material orders and the absence of actual consumption data from Boeing, GAO found it reasonable for AFMC to reflect this increase in its treatment of material consumption. The evaluation found that contract administration and oversight cost $5.5 million and estimated contractor award fees of $5.2 million.

---

[3]An updated cost study showed the cost difference between government and private operation of the facility to be more than 20 percent (private communication from Air Force Installation and Logistics (AF/IL), dated 8 November 1999).

Boeing questioned AFMC's assessment, stating that Boeing's estimate was about $6.8 million lower than costs before privatization-in-place. Boeing also noted that it is exceeding contract quality requirements and minimum delivery schedules. The Air Force believed Boeing's cost analysis incomplete. For example, Boeing's estimate did not include contract administration and oversight costs of about $3.4 million, and it overstated historic operations and maintenance costs by about $5 million.

U.S. GAO (1997b) found that the AFMC interim study was methodologically sound and that it used the best available data, but GAO notes that this is an interim analysis and actual costs will not be known until the data are available.

CASE STUDY: SINGLE CONTRACTS FOR MULTIPLE SUPPORT SERVICES[4]

Participants

Public: Base/military installation

Private: Private, for-profit entity

Background

Base operations support services are functions necessary to support, operate, and maintain DoD installations. The military services differ in their definitions of base support services making it difficult to determine the actual size and cost of this workforce, but DoD estimates that base support activities cost more than $30 billion in FY 1997. Increasingly, DoD is outsourcing commercially available support services (U.S. GAO, 1998).

Because of Congressional interest in potential savings that could be achieved by using a single contract, rather than several smaller contracts, to encompass multiple base operations, GAO surveyed existing single contracts for multiple services. GAO found that the decision to use a single contract occurred either as a result of an A-76

---

[4]This case draws heavily upon U.S. GAO (1998).

study or at the time the installation or its current mission was established. At the installations surveyed, not all base operations support requirements were met through the single contract. Rather, installations relied on some combination of single contract for multiple services, single contracts for specific services, regional contracts for specific services, and the use of in-house personnel. The types of services procured under the multiple service contracts vary depending on the mission and functions of the installation, missions of tenant activities, existing contractual arrangements, legislative restrictions, and a desire to keep some functions in house (U.S. GAO, 1998).

Contract Provisions

Most of these contracts are fixed-price-award-fee contracts that place maximum risk on the contractor and minimum risk on the government. For example, Naval Submarine Base Bangor awarded a ten-year multiple support services contract to Johnson Controls World Services, Inc., in 1997. The contract is a fixed-price-award-fee contract for a base price of about $40 million annually. The contract provides a wide range of base support services including administrative support, various public works services, utility and supply services, and security services. It contains provisions for Johnson Controls World Services, Inc., to meet ISO 9000 standards to better ensure they can meet customer requirements and help reduce the monitoring costs.

Major Facilitating Factors

The types of services procured under multiple service contracts are influenced by the mission and functions of the installation, missions of tenant activities, existing contractual arrangements, legislative restrictions, and a desire to keep some functions in-house. Individuals having implemented such contracts stress that a well-defined performance work statement improves the contract's success (U.S. GAO, 1998).

Major Constraining Factors

Although some small businesses do compete in single multiple service contracts, concern remains that it is difficult for them to compete because of the high cost of preparing proposals and the low probability of winning the contract when competing with large businesses. The effect on small businesses is a concern for DoD because of a requirement, contained in the Small Business Administration Reauthorization Act of 1997, that federal agencies consider the impact on small businesses' ability to compete when considering consolidating activities previously performed by small businesses into multiple services contracts (U.S. GAO, 1998).

Results

Although contracting officials report efficiency gains, including reduced overhead, cross utilization of contract personnel, and increased flexibility, cost savings from single contracts are not documented. At most of the installations, savings cannot be easily quantified because there is no requirement to track savings. Further, contracts have changed since the initial commercial activities studies were completed, so little basis for comparative analysis exists (U.S. GAO, 1998).

CASE STUDY: NAVY AVIATION MAINTENANCE CONTRACT, TA-4J SKYHAWKS[5]

Participants

Public: U.S. Navy

Private: Lockheed, Grumman, and UNC Aviation Services

Background

Maintenance work for the organizational- and intermediate-level maintenance of the A-4s and the T-2 Buckeyes that are flown by the

---

[5]This case draws heavily upon Tighe et al. (1997).

training commands was competed in an A-76 competition in the mid-1980s. The winning bid for the A-76 competition was about 20 percent lower than the in-house bid, after contract management and competition costs were included.

The conversion to contract maintenance began in July 1986 with Training Wing Two and concluded in June 1988 with Training Wing Six. The aircraft maintenance has been competed three times and three different contractors have won each competition. Lockheed won the initial bid, Grumman the second, and UNC Aviation Services the third.

Contract Provisions

The contract covers the organizational- and intermediate-level maintenance of the A-4s and T-2 Buckeyes that are flown by the training commands. It is a fixed-price contract for one base year plus four option years.

Results

The Center for Naval Analyses (CNA) conducted a study to determine if the change to outsourced maintenance was beneficial or detrimental to the quality of aircraft maintenance provided to the training commands. CNA compared the quality and cost of in-house and contracted maintenance of the TA-4J Skyhawk aircraft. This jet was chosen because data existed for both in-house and contracted maintenance. CNA used fully mission capable (the percentage of time the aircraft is fully ready, with no system degradations) and mission capable (percentage of time the aircraft is ready to fly, and not degraded by system discrepancies) as quality measures and direct maintenance man-hours per flight hour (the amount of organizational-level maintenance completed for every flight hour) as a cost measure (Tighe et al., 1997).

CNA found that after the initial contract went into effect, there was a long break-in period during which the contractor's performance was lower than the previous performance of in-house personnel. It was almost four years before the contractor reached the mean level and two years before the contractor's performance began to improve.

Thus, for two to four years, training commands suffered a reduced mission-capable rate (Tighe et al., 1997).

After the break-in period, the contractor met or exceeded the previous in-house level of quality and did so using fewer resources. The contractor provided an equivalent amount of flight hours with a 33 percent reduction in direct maintenance man-hours, reducing costs and saving resources. Interestingly, no break-in period was observed when one contractor took over from another. The cost savings continued in subsequent contracts, even with a change in contractors (Tighe et al., 1997).

CASE STUDY: THE U.K. INLAND REVENUE SERVICE[6]

Participants

Public: U.K. Inland Revenue Service

Private: EDS

Background

The objectives of the Inland Revenue Service were to bring about faster implementation of new tax systems, increase its national compliance rate, and decrease its operational costs. They entered into a ten-year risk/reward contract with EDS for tax systems modernization in July 1994. This contract called for outsourcing of all information-technology-related services that support tax assessment and collection. EDS assumed operational responsibility for 11 computer data centers and successfully transitioned over 1,900 employees to EDS. In July 1995, the Inland Revenue Service asked EDS to assume technical responsibility for the development of the Self Assessment Tax system, touted as one of the major reforms in the U.K. taxation system. In January 1996, EDS took over responsibility for application development including product delivery, process management, and productivity. As a result, they transitioned an additional 1,000 civil service employees to EDS, including the Application Development Team. EDS initiated a tactical improvement program

---

[6]This case draws heavily upon materials supplied by EDS.

for the entire joint team, which included a performance metrics program and adoption of its corporate standards for project management and its Systems Life Cycle methodology as the development standard.

Major Facilitating Factors

The major drivers on the part of the Inland Revenue Service to outsource were to improve service to citizens, increase revenues, and control costs. For example, the contract promised savings of £225 million over the lifetime of the contract. The second was EDS's agreement to transition all affected civil service employees at comparable pay and benefit levels. Another important factor was clear specification of performance metrics with which to measure EDS's performance: quality of service, customer service, timeliness of performance, cost control. In addition, the Inland Revenue Service's willingness to treat EDS as a partner and to have an EDS representative participate in senior board level meetings was an important factor contributing to the success of the partnership, along with the shared risk and reward nature of the relationship.

EDS has identified a number of factors critical to the success of such partnerships:

- Enterprise plan, sponsorship, and buy-in
- Stakeholder involvement
- Procurement must support goals
- Flexibility to change roles as requirements change
- Requirements management plan
- Accurate project progress visibility
- Single responsibility for integration
- Transformation and change management expertise and plans
- Availability of experienced skill base and resources
- Appropriate incentives

- Ability to achieve private and public sector success

- Appreciation for cultural differences (O'Malley, 1999)

Major Constraining Factors

Opposition from the staff association was the major constraining factor. They had questions asked in Parliament, mounted a vigorous lobbying campaign, and warned about the dangers of tax data in the hands of an American private company.

Results

As of June 1997, the Inland Revenue reported that one million self-assessment tax forms were filed and only 5 percent had to be returned to taxpayers. Further, the Inland Revenue's computer systems performed very well (*Financial Times*, June 19, 1997). In addition, EDS reports that cost savings from this partnership amount to 15–20 percent of Inland Revenue's current IT costs or $300 million in savings to date. EDS maintains an open book arrangement and has profit shared every year on IT cost savings. EDS has hit or exceeded targets with respect to quality of service and customer service every year, and EDS staff have received awards for design and usability of their ideas/processes. Employee turnover has been less than 5 percent since 1994.

Notes

- For an opposing point of view, see Davies (undated). He cites a study by Wilcocks of Templeton College, Oxford, which analyzed 61 outsourcing deals in Europe and the United States; the expected savings did not materialize or were invisible (including several deals of the EDS/U.K. Inland Revenue Service type). The greatest chance of failure came from long-term contracts in which all IT was outsourced.

- There is a great deal of concern about privacy issues, with this much information in the hands of a private contractor.

- There is also concern about the way in which a private contractor could hold the government for ransom, should they decide to go with another contractor.

CASE STUDY: THE BRITISH ARMY LOGISTICS INFORMATION SYSTEMS AGENCY[7]

Participants

Public: The British Army Logistics Information Systems Agency

Private: EDS

Background

One of the U.K. Ministry of Defence's priorities is to modernize IT services and to provide the most effective logistical support to the British Army. LISA detailed several key business goals including a detailed examination of processes and redesign of these, where needed; adoption of best practices in the delivery of IT services; design of a structured approach to logistics system modernization; and consolidation and outsourcing of existing systems. In December 1995, EDS won a five-year contract to provide a complete range of IT services to LISA. EDS currently provides all IT services, business process reengineering, systems development, and modernization, and also operates two GOCO data centers.

Major Facilitating Factors

The major facilitating factors included the department's desire to become more cost-effective and to modernize, EDS's reputation as a leader in IT and in building private-public partnerships, and EDS's assimilation of former government workers into the EDS workforce. EDS transferred 180 government personnel to EDS.

---

[7]This case draws heavily upon materials supplied by EDS.

Results

The partnership has resulted in $30 million of documented savings with more expected as planned improvements are implemented with no degradation in service as a result of EDS taking over the strategic logistics system.   EDS has completed the Year 2000 requirements analysis; implemented a commercial-off-the-shelf (COTS)-based financial management system; and improved system responsiveness with the migration of ammunition management and asset tracking systems to modern platforms.

Chapter Twelve

EMPLOYEE STOCK OWNERSHIP PLAN

Provider	Private
Staffing	Private
Customers	Government and private
Source of funding	Direct appropriation
Distinctive features	Employees of the organization and outside investors own the business; any firm can create an ESOP
Implementation issues	• ESOPs can be created only in the absence of A-76
	• Government must decide to "get out of the business" and spin the business out of government to form a profit or nonprofit company
Pros	• Employee ownership is seen as a way to provide employees with a direct financial incentive in the privatization transaction; this offers opportunities for significant capital ownership and the potential for career enhancement
	• Guarantees of employment may help mitigate concerns regarding job security
	• Because of the economic incentive, improved efficiencies and cost reductions in the provision of the service may result
	• Successful privatization through employee ownership may facilitate the expansion of products and services
	• Tax advantages are offered by the ESOP to the lending institution
Cons	• There are up-front administrative costs when establishing an ESOP—even a mid-sized ESOP can cost $50,000 in initial legal, accounting, actuarial, and appraisal fees; annual administrative costs are likely to be over $10,000 per year; only activities with a minimum payroll of over $500,000 should be considered for an ESOP

Cons (cont.)	• Care needs to be exercised in ensuring compliance with conflict-of-interest laws and ethical rules; government employees are prohibited from having a financial interest in the outcome of decisions in which they are involved or in making use of inside information in their private financial undertakings; thus, protecting employees who are considering an ESOP initiative from conflict-of-interest laws is essential; this can be achieved by making sure that negotiations are carried out by a trustee or representative and not by the employees themselves • Careful financial planning needed • Need to define a new relationship between the government and the new contracting company, including setting up of performance goals and compliance with ESOP-related provisions of the contract • Need a buy-in from employees who traditionally are very concerned with job security, pay and benefits, and personal belief in public versus private employment.
Examples	Amtrak is being considered
Case study	U.S. Investigations Services, Inc.

CASE STUDY: U. S. INVESTIGATIONS SERVICES, INC.

Participants

Public: Office of Personnel Management (OPM)

Private: USIS

Background

OPM, following the mandates of the National Performance Review and the Workforce Restructuring Act, wished to downsize OPM and focus on their core mission. As one of the many reforms undertaken, OPM decided to stop conducting investigations in-house. OPM presented their investigations unit, which conducted government background investigations, with several options. One of these was to form an employee stock ownership plan—a new employee-owned company that would perform many of the same services, albeit in the private sector. USIS was created in 1996. OPM was highly supportive throughout the transition and bore the costs associated with the feasibility analysis and the subsequent implementation of the plan.

Even more important, it awarded the fledgling company a three-year exclusive contract to conduct investigations for OPM. This was the first government privatization of its kind in the United States. Of the 706 employees who were offered jobs with the new company, 681 accepted the offer. They received equivalent salaries and benefits as well as ownership of 90 percent of the company through an ESOP. Four outside managers were brought in to head the company and they each made an investment for the remaining 10 percent of the equity.

Major Facilitating Factors

The commitment and support of OPM and underwriting of initial costs by OPM played a major role in getting USIS started. OPM awarded a three-year exclusive contract to protect the fledgling company and to get it off the ground. Other important factors were hiring outside managers to run the company, equipment transfers at low cost, and the appointment of an outside ESOP trustee. This latter ensured that no conflict-of-interest laws were violated during the time the contract was being negotiated.

Major Constraining Factors

The one major constraining factor was the fear of employees and unions about loss of jobs and benefits.

Results

A private consulting firm estimated that USIS would save the taxpayers $25 million in five years, although there do not appear to be any studies of the actual cost savings.

Chapter Thirteen

ASSET SALE

Provider	Private
Staffing	Private
Customers	Private or government
Source of funding	N/A
Distinctive features	Government "gets out of the business" and sells its assets
Implementation issues	GSA disposal process
Pros	• Provides selling entity money from the sale • Enables unused government resources to be used in the private sector
Cons	GSA disposal process is lengthy
Examples	• New York-New Jersey Port Authority sold the Vista Hotel • Michigan sold its Workers Compensation Accident Fund
Case studies	Hamilton land sales

CASE STUDY: HAMILTON LAND SALES[1]

Participants

Public: GSA and Navy

Private: New Hamilton Partnership (GSA parcel), Novato, California

Background

In 1974, Hamilton Air Force Base, located in the City of Novato in Marin County, California, was decommissioned. Subsequently, the

---

[1]This case draws heavily upon State of California (undated).

base was divided into three areas. The airfield, 722 acres, was transferred to the Army; the housing and recreational facilities, 554 acres, were transferred to the Navy; and the remaining 411 acre parcel was transferred to GSA. In 1985, GSA offered the parcel for public sale. The 1998 BRAC closed the Army airfield, and the Navy vacated the housing in 1996 because of a BRAC 1993 closure of the Navy's San Francisco bases.

Provisions of Asset Sales[2]

GSA Parcel. The GSA property was sold to Berg-Revoir development group in 1985. Berg-Revoir bid $45 million for the property based on a plan for a high-density housing development. The developer planned to build 2,500–3,500 housing units and 3 million square feet of commercial space. However, the community strongly objected to this plan and overturned it by community referendum. The referendum in combination with the discovery of a landfill on the property led the original buyer to sell his option on the property.

The new option holder, the Martin Group (later becoming the New Hamilton Partnership), worked for four years with the community to develop a plan for a reduced level of development that included 955 single-family detached homes and duplexes, 95 units of affordable rental housing for the elderly, 535,000 square feet of commercial and retail space, and 200 acres of open land and recreation area. The reduced level of development dictated a lower sales price. In 1993, the community was successful in having federal legislation enacted to reduce the sales price from $45 to $15 million. In 1995, 150 acres in the first phase of the sale were conveyed to the New Hamilton Partnership for $18 million.

Phase 1 of the sale has an approved Environmental Impact Report and a plan approved by the city. After remediation, phase 2 of the GSA parcel includes 250 acres that were conveyed to Novato in July 1997 by a long-term lease for $1. The developer will purchase portions of the property slated for residential, office, and retail use.

---

[2]This case reports on the asset sale activities of the Hamilton Army Airfield. The entirety of the reuse is not described.

Navy Parcel. On August 18, 1998, the Novato City Council approved an offer to purchase 554 acres for $8.13 million. Seventy-five percent of the Navy property at Hamilton contains nearly 1,000 housing units built in the 1950s. Nearly 60 percent of the units will be rebuilt or retrofitted as affordable housing in compliance with the community's homeless assistance plan. The affordable housing component of the Hamilton Reuse Plan meets the federal requirement that a negotiated sale offer an "appreciable public benefit" not available through a public sale.

Negotiations for the sale took nearly three years because of differing appraisals of the property. A recent agreement between the two parties on appraisal assumptions, including the build-out time-frame for redeveloping the property, consideration of building codes, and demolition and construction costs, resulted in appraisals that fell within a reasonable range of one another. An estimated $1.6 million cost to remediate asbestos on the property was deducted from the $8.13 million sale price.

Novato will issue a request for qualification (RFQ) for a master developer in 1999.

Major Facilitating and Constraining Factors

The community was extremely influential in determining the reuse of the Hamilton property. The community effectively blocked Berg-Revoir's high-density development plan of the GSA property. The Marin community possesses a strong slow-growth attitude, partly because of heavy traffic on the Rt. 101 corridor and environmental constraints on nondeveloped properties. Only after the second developer worked with the community for four years was development of the GSA property permitted.

The differences in the assumptions of the original Navy and city appraisals slowed their negotiation process. Although both appraisals originally took into consideration the reuse plan and were based on the highest and best use to obtain the fair market value of the property, it was not until the city and Navy agreed on certain basic assumptions, such as the build-out time-frame for redeveloping the property, that the appraisals fell into range of one another (State of California, undated).

ISSUES RELATED TO COMPETITIVE SOURCING

In 1995, the Commission on Roles and Missions of the Armed Forces (CORM) focused on expanded outsourcing and privatization (O&P) as the most important policy tool to improve the cost-effectiveness of DoD support activities. In 1996, the Defense Science Board Task Force on Outsourcing and Privatization called for a revolution in DoD business affairs to support the revolution in military affairs. It concluded that DoD could save $10 billion or more a year through expanded O&P.

It is important to get some definitions clear at the outset. First, competitive sourcing is fundamentally different from "contracting-out." DoD already contracts-out for many support services. For example, contracting-out already accounts for about 25 percent of the billets classified by the Air Force as "commercial" or potentially available from the private sector. The other services would show similar numbers, although the actual activities outsourced differ. "Competitive sourcing" is what the DRI and other recent commissions have focused on. It is an incremental expansion of support activities bought from external sources. As CNA (Tighe et al., 1997) has argued repeatedly, the principal advantage of competitive sourcing comes from competition itself. Whether DoD or a contractor wins, DoD still benefits significantly in a typical competition. So this is more about competition than outsourcing.

Second, privatization is the second half of what was once called O&P and is now called competitive sourcing and privatization (CS&P). It is primarily about inducing private firms to finance new housing and utility services for DoD. It includes some transfer of DoD assets to the private sector but almost always in the context of a broader program to get more investment in housing and utilities. This is where the most innovative activity is going on in DoD to expand dependence on external sources. This is not "privatization" in the usual sense of the word.

This appendix focuses on competitive sourcing. Two versions of competitive sourcing are relevant to DoD—A-76 studies and depot-level competitions. The latter are often referred to as public/private competitions for depot-level maintenance and have had the most public visibility over the last two years as the Air Force competed immense maintenance workloads in San Antonio and Sacramento. We primarily focus on A-76 cost competitions in this appendix.

CONTRACTING THROUGH A-76 COST COMPETITIONS

The policy of using commercial suppliers for inherently commercial activities in the government in the post World War II era dates back to the Bureau of the Budget Bulletins issued in the middle 1950s and early 1960s. In this era, concerns were raised over the government's competing with the private sector and the adverse effect of this on economic growth. These policy concerns are articulated in the OMB Circular No. A-76 along with concern over an added issue—that of enhancing productivity of in-house efforts. Under the latest A-76 circular, if an activity qualifies as a commercial activity and DoD cannot justify keeping the activity in-house for policy reasons, then a cost comparison will be made between the bid of a commercial supplier and the cost estimate for providing the activity in-house. Table A.1 lists the conditions permitting either government or commercial performance of commercial activities. Careful attention in the circular is paid to defining functions that qualify as commercial rather than inherently governmental. A-76 applies only to Executive Branch agencies and organizations, and Congress explicitly exempts several activities in these agencies.

If an activity qualifies as a commercial activity and is not exempted by any of the special provisions, the circular and its supplemental handbook describe a process for determining whether or not a commercial activity should be conducted by an in-house team or by an outside contractor. The first step in this process is to establish a baseline for the activity that is to be considered. The second step is to develop a performance work statement (PWS) that defines the overall services to be provided and provides in great detail the workload process maps and flowcharts. The third step is to formally advertise for competitive bidding by outside organizations. As part of that process, the in-house agency or group can reform itself into an MEO to compete. The MEO is the government's best estimate of the organizational structure and needed resources that meet the requirements of the PWS at the lowest cost. The supplemental handbook to the circular gives detailed instructions on how to assemble the in-house cost estimates. To win a competition, a private sector bid must be at least 10 percent lower than the public sector bid.

Benefits and Costs of Cost Competitions

A managed cost competition offers three main advantages (Tighe et al., 1997):

- It provides cost visibility; often, this is the first time that decisionmakers realize the full cost of performing that function;

- It provides choice as to who should perform that function;

- It promotes efficiency and lower cost, regardless of who wins the competition.

The first item, although undoubtedly true, rests on the assumption that all costs can be correctly identified and assessed. If not, the competition is unlikely to provide full cost visibility. Even in such a case, however, the process of the competition itself is likely to provide much more information on costs than would otherwise perhaps be available.

Studies by Savas (1992), Marcus (1993), and Tighe et al. (1997) have shown that there is a significant potential for savings and other improvements from competition and outsourcing. Indeed, the 1997 Quadrennial Defense Review reports that between 1979 and 1994, DoD conducted over 2,000 competitions, of which about half were won by the in-house team. Annual operating costs were reduced by 31 percent, resulting in cumulative savings of $1.5 billion a year (DoD, 1997, p. 29). These are impressive results.

Table A.1
Governmental Versus Contract Performance of Commercial Activities

Conditions Permitting Government Performance of Commercial Activities

National Defense or Intelligence Security. The Secretary of Defense, or designee, approves national defense justifications. The Director of Central Intelligence, or designee, approves national security justifications.

Patient Care. Commercial activities at government-owned hospitals or other health facilities may be performed by in-house, Inter Service Support Agreement (ISSA) or contract employees when needed to maintain the quality of direct patient care.

Core Capability. A core capability of in-house and contract resources may be war-ranted for certain functional areas.

Research and Development. Research and development activities may be converted to or from in-house, contract, or ISSA without cost comparison. Severable support activities are subject to the cost comparison provisions of this supplement.

No Satisfactory Commercial Source Available. Agencies will solicit private sector interest and certify that the solicitation did not restrict or otherwise limit competition.

Functions with 10 or Fewer Full-Time Equivalent (FTE). May be converted to or from in-house, contract or ISSA without a cost comparison, if the contracting officer determines that reasonable prices cannot otherwise be obtained.

Meet Performance Standard. Agencies may demonstrate that the activity meets or exceeds generally recognized industry cost and performance standards, after all adjustments required by this supplement.

Lower Cost. Results of a cost comparison demonstrate that in-house performance is less costly.

Temporary Authorization. Temporary emergency performance may be warranted not to exceed the next full contract option year.

However, there are significant costs associated with these competitions in terms of time and effort. Those completed have typically taken two years (and often much longer) to complete. In addition, Keating (1997) points out that since 1978, approximately five A-76 cost comparisons have been canceled for every eight completed. Controlling for other factors, cost comparisons that were more vulnerable to cancellations are those involving functions with large number of civilians, in the Marine Corps, in the Defense Logistics Agency, or in education and training and manufacturing activities.

Table A.1 (cont.)

Conditions Permitting Contract Performance of Commercial Activities
Contracted Activities. Should be obtained by contract, unless a cost comparison demonstrates that in-house or ISSA performance is more cost effective.
New Requirement. Should be obtained by contract, unless contract quality or price appear unreasonable. A cost comparison is performed to convert the activity to in-house or ISSA performance.
Severable Expansions. Same as above.
ISSAs. Commercial activities should not be performed through new or expanded ISSAs, except as provided by law or this supplement.
Activities with 10 or Fewer FTE. May be converted to or from in-house, contract or ISSA, without a cost comparison.
Activities with 11 or More FTE. May be converted to contract or ISSA, without cost comparison, if fair and reasonable contract prices can be obtained by competitive award and all directly affected federal employees on permanent appointments can be reassigned to other comparable federal positions.
Preferential Procurement Programs. Contract performance may be granted, without cost comparison, if the contract is awarded to a preferential procurement program.
Lower Cost. Conversion to contract is required if a cost comparison indicates that contract performance is the lower cost alternative.

SOURCE: This table is taken from OMB-Circular A-76. Any reference in the table to "this supplement" refers to OMB-Circular A-76.

In addition, several were canceled because they had reached the two-year limit that first appeared in the FY1991 Appropriations Act. The act specified that single function cost comparisons that had not reached bid opening after two years must be canceled.

In another study, Keating, Camm, and Hanks (1998) used Air Force data, current as of July 1, 1996, from the Commercial Activity Management Information System (CAMIS) to analyze trends in competition cancellations. They found that approximately three initiatives have been canceled for every seven completed. Results suggest that, controlling for other factors, multifunction initiatives are more likely to be completed than single-function initiatives. Among the commands, the Air Education and Training Command (AETC) had the greatest success in completing A-76 initiatives. Among the functions, social services, real property maintenance, and installation services initiatives are most likely to be completed whereas education and training initiatives have been especially vulnerable to cancellation.

Tighe et al. (1997) note that the A-76 process itself can be used to delay progress if managerial resistance exists. For instance, one competition lasted eight years before it was cancelled in 1991 by Congressional moratorium. During the eight years, the functional manager delayed the study by bundling and unbundling the functions every few years. In a different competition, staff prevented source selection by changing the contract type five times.

The median cost comparison (between 1978 and 1994) took 664 days to the initial decision, the mean was 810 days, and over 10 percent of completed cost comparisons took at least four years to the initial decision. Tighe et al. (undated) point out that initial competition costs averaged 11 percent of baseline costs, whereas recurring costs to monitor contracts averaged something below 10 percent (pp. 5–6).

An A-76 cost competition is, of course, not the only way to outsource a function or activity. This could be done directly either through a formal bidding process where outside bidders are invited to bid for the work or through the selection of a sole source provider. We turn now to the benefits and costs of outsourcing in general.

Making Cost Competitions More Effective

Tighe et al. (undated) offer detailed suggestions on making managed cost competitions more effective. To minimize transitory problems during the initial learning curve period, they suggest:

- Using negotiated competitions that take bidders' past performance into account and performance-based contracts;

- Integrating contract and technical people into a team—problems arise because technical people write the contract but the contract personnel monitor it;

- Putting in place good employee transition plans; and

- Writing enforceable contracts.

In terms of implementing the A-76 process, they suggest:

- Increasing the size and scope of competitions, providing training for local managers, and rewarding those undertaking competitions;

- Holding in-house teams to the same cost accounting rules and regulations as private contractors;

- Screening out unqualified bidders;

- Bundling functions together; and

- Executing an MOU that specifies the work to be performed, its quality, and cost, when an in-house team wins.

Senior DoD officials pointed out that two of these are already done in the A-76 process: In-house contractors are held to the same cost accounting rules and regulations as private contractors and an MOU is executed when the in-house team wins (although the MOU is perhaps not enforced as stringently as it could or should be).

Present RAND research verifies that most of these recommendations are compatible with best commercial practice (Pint and Baldwin, 1997; Moore et al., 1999, 1997, 1996; Camm and Moore, 1997).

Recognizing the constraints placed on this process by federal procurement policies discussed above, they also suggest statutory relief of the following:

- The "60-40" split, by which DoD is required by statute (10 USC Section 2466) to perform 60 percent of depot maintenance in public depots;[1]

- The "core" maintenance rule (10 USC Sections 2464 and 2469), which requires DoD to keep "core" maintenance capabilities in-house;

---

[1]The "60–40" split has been changed to "50–50," which would imply a greater percentage of work available to be competed. However, definitions also changed at the same time so it is unclear what the effect of the new rule has been.

- Davis-Bacon and Service Contracting Acts, which specify wage rates and impose administrative tasks on contractors;[2] and

- Title 10 USC Section 2465, which requires that fire-fighting and security functions be performed by government personnel.[3]

BENEFITS AND COSTS OF USING EXTERNAL SOURCES FOR SERVICES[4]

Quite apart from managed competitions, more general rewards and risks associated with outsourcing are important to understand. The benefits are widely known:

- Lower cost: this is the primary reason for DoD's interest;

- Improved performance: using specialist providers, organizations can improve responsiveness, quality, reliability, and flexibility of their support services;

- Improved focus on core competencies: For example, by outsourcing desktop support, Microsoft was able to call on the superior call center operations and management information systems of Entex;

- Quicker access to innovation: firms providing support services survive by keeping up to date. Organic support services not subject to continuous benchmarking can often be more complacent about new developments.

There are numerous examples of successful outsourcing. One is the U.K. Inland Revenue Service's decision to enter into a ten-year risk/reward contract with EDS for tax systems modernization in July

---

[2]A senior DoD official commented that it would be difficult, if not impossible, to obtain waivers of these rules.

[3]Other requirements as well render conversion to contractor performance unwieldy. For example, Section 2461 of 10 USC Chapter 146 requires that DoD conduct a detailed cost analysis of any commercial or industrial type function involving more than a minimum number of employees, if it is considering contracting out that function to the private sector. Senior DoD officials are concerned about what this means for reverse A-76 competitions (in which the private sector won the original bid, but which DoD is now considering bringing back in house).

[4]This section draws heavily on Camm and Moore (1997).

1994.[5] This contract called for outsourcing all IT-related services that support tax assessment and collection. The results are impressive: a 50 percent decrease in the number of returns with errors, cost savings of 15–20 percent of Inland Revenue's current IT costs, and very low employee turnover (less than 5 percent since 1994). However, as Kettl (1993) warns:

> Government's relationships with the private sector are not self-administering; they require, rather, aggressive management by a strong, competent government (pp. 5–6).

Camm and Moore (1997) offer an excellent summary of the risks associated with outsourcing a DoD function:

- A catastrophic failure to perform: For example, a recent DoD air delivery contractor was late 40 percent of the time, forcing DoD to go through the lengthy process of contract termination and renegotiation;

- Loss of real-time control: real-time control of a complex process becomes more important, especially in an uncertain operating environment;

- High transaction costs associated with some activities: Some activities may be so subtle as to make it difficult to specify clearly what is needed. This leads to high transaction costs as work statements are renegotiated and this may be unacceptable when time is of the essence, as in combat;

- Inadequate investments in customized assets: providers will not make customized investments unless they believe that they can get a positive return on them.

- Loss of needed skills: For example, if DoD decides to outsource the activity, it must provide aggressive oversight of the outsourced activity and also make certain that the activity is fully integrated with DoD's planning, execution, and information systems. Thus, in common with many companies in the private sector, it may pay DoD to keep the activity in house to train

---

[5]For further details, see Chapter Eleven.

managers who will oversee contract sources of this activity later in their career.[6]

Examples abound to show that outsourcing does not guarantee high performance. This can only be brought about by good contracting and good selection. Contractual difficulties in outsourcing work (Pint and Baldwin, 1997) include asset specificity, function complexity or uncertainty, and measurement problems. Often, the difficulty in specifying the work or estimating the workload can lead to poor performance. For example, in the early 1990s, the Florida state government had contracted with EDS to build an automated Social Security system. In the first year, the system had problems, causing massive logjams of cases and paying out $100 million more than it should have in benefits. The state stopped paying EDS and EDS sued, claiming that the state had changed the system unexpectedly and underestimated the amount of information it needed to process.

It is clear from DoD's own experience that not all private sector firms offer high performance. In addition, performance gains are usually greater if outsourcing leverages *existing* capacity and capabilities. DoD's outsourcings are unlikely to yield the best net benefits if they do not directly access the highest performing providers. However, until recently, federal procurement policies and regulations often made this difficult.

CURRENT FEDERAL PROCUREMENT POLICY

Federal procurement policy is based on three key principles: equity, integrity, and efficiency (Kelman, 1990). Equity concerns discourage any effort to restrict the qualifications of private sector providers and seek to give preference to small businesses and those owned by disadvantaged groups. To maintain high integrity, the government seeks to prevent *all* fraud and abuse by government employees and contractors. Such efforts generated extraordinarily detailed and burdensome procurement rules that often impose larger costs than they

---

[6]A senior DoD official commented that merely keeping the activity in house may not guarantee that the agency will foster or retain the skills needed for excellent contract administration and smart buying. It is important to deliberately foster and train managers in these skills.

avoid. To promote efficiency, the government often placed emphasis on the minimally qualified source that offered the lowest cost.
Risk-averse contract personnel were often reluctant to use other criteria.

Recognizing these problems, recent acquisition reform efforts have
sought to simplify the rules for negotiated acquisitions (Federal Acquisition Regulation, Part 15). These efforts have tried to minimize
the complexity of the solicitation, evaluation, and selection process,
while still trying to maintain fairness and equity and ensuring that
the government gets the best value for its money. Other similar efforts are under way.

STRATEGIC SOURCING: THE KEY TO THE FUTURE?[7]

Innovative commercial firms are shifting to something they refer to
as "strategic sourcing." These firms are looking for partners, not
vendors—partners that complement the core competencies of the
buying firms. Buyers expect lower costs from such partnerships but
they are more interested in improvements over time than in current
costs. Indeed, the business literature emphasizes that cost reduction
should not be the primary criterion used in outsourcing. More effective criteria include strategic focus, better performance, accelerating
re-engineering, and sharing risks with the supplier (Pint and Baldwin, 1997). These eventually lead to lower costs.

Adopting such a broad, strategic view increases the potential for outsourcing large classes of activities. In the private sector, as partnerships have deepened and the suppliers and purchasers have "co-
evolved," the bundles considered in specific sourcing decisions have
grown to include both more activities and more discretion about
how to provide services. This allows the suppliers to become more
efficient by exploiting economies of scale and scope. Innovative
firms have come to understand that source selection and contracting
are themselves core competencies that the buyer must cultivate and
improve over time. They pay more attention to the sourcing process
and put into place formal processes with formal quality tools to drive

---

[7]This section is drawn from Camm and Moore (1997).

continuous improvement in the process itself (Camm and Moore, 1997).

However, by and large, in the past, the outsourcing process in DoD largely maintained the old focus. Decisions have been made primarily at the local level for tactical reasons, the typical provider has been an arm's-length vendor who performed specific tasks under very specific directions of a performance work statement,[8] they have typically chosen the lowest cost source, no consistent service-wide sourcing policy has emerged, and most outsourcings have been small and involved narrow functions (Camm and Moore, 1997).

This is beginning to change. In the name of applying acquisition reform to service contracts, the senior leadership of DoD favors performance-based service contracting that employs best-value competitions to choose better external providers. The contracting community of the Air force, for example, now thinks of itself strategically as the "business advisor" to the warfighters and other customers who use the services that the Air Force buys. DoD's challenge is now to implement this kind of vision in the field. Successful implementation will require fundamental changes in the skills, attitudes, and behavior of the DoD contracting, financial management, and other functional personnel responsible for buying services for DoD from external sources. Camm (1996) and Camm and Moore (1997) offer some sensible and more general thoughts on how to enhance the success of strategic sourcing efforts:

- Plan formally for major organizational changes required to implement and sustain strategic sourcing;

- Focus on improving requirements determination and contract design;

- Start with the best candidate activities for sourcing review;

- Where necessary, protect constituents that outsourcing might hurt or seek constructive ways to diffuse opposition (Camm and Moore, 1997, pp. xxii–xxiii).

---

[8]Interestingly, commercial firms often refer to this as "outtasking" not "outsourcing."

To garner support, they suggest framing change to the degree of senior support available, having the organization designated a special pilot, building a coalition of parties involved, using metrics relevant to parties affected to support change, and providing incentives to the parties involved. Baldwin, Camm, and Moore (1998) stress the importance of developing and using metrics to justify investments, measure ultimate success, and to support incentives.

Camm and Moore (1997) also outline a strategic sourcing process:

- Identify activities available for sourcing review;

- Identify DoD organizations responsible for review;

- Rank activities for review:

  - Highest priority: generic business and administrative activities, especially activities that commercial firms currently outsource and that are currently provided by robust, commercial supplier industries;

  - High priority: logistics activities that do not depend on access to technical data from the original equipment manufacturer and that many high-quality firms routinely supply to other firms;

  - High priority (subject to resolution of important political risks): activities that the DoD members consume directly for their own personal care such as housing, commissaries, and medical and dental care.

- Conduct initial analysis to refine approach and identify likely source: need a simple, agile, robust analytic process such as those used by commercial firms to compare options systematically and creatively;

- Finalize work scope and select source;

- Manage source to execute mission and improve process: ensure an effective handoff and integration of the new source effectively into its own planning and management process.

DoD already implements some of these steps (for example, steps 1 and 2) but some may be hard to do, given the rules and regulations of A-76. Nonetheless, strategic sourcing, although requiring bold and innovative steps to implement, may fit in well with the current reform efforts to foster a revolution in business affairs.

GLOSSARY[1]

Asset Sale
    An asset sale is the transfer of ownership of government assets, commercial type enterprises, or functions to the private sector. In general, the government will have no role in the financial support, management, or oversight of a sold asset. However, if the asset is sold to a company in an industry with monopolistic characteristics, the government may regulate certain aspects of the business, such as the regulation of utility rates.

Competition
    Competition occurs when two or more parties independently attempt to secure the business of a customer by offering the most favorable terms. Competition in relation to government activities is usually categorized in three ways: (1) public versus private, in which public-sector organizations compete with the private sector to conduct public-sector business; (2) public versus public, in which public-sector organizations compete among themselves to conduct public-sector business; and (3) private versus private, in which private-sector organizations compete among themselves to conduct public-sector business.

---

[1]This glossary is taken from U.S. GAO (1997a).

Contracting Out	Contracting out is the hiring of private-sector firms or nonprofit organizations to provide a good or service for the government. Under this approach, the government remains the financier and has management and policy control over the type and quality of services to be provided. Thus, the government can replace contractors that do not perform well.
Divestiture	Divestiture involves the sale of government-owned assets or commercial-type functions or enterprises. After the divestiture, the government generally has no role concerning financial support, management, regulation, or oversight.
Employee Stock Owner-ship Plans	Under an employee stock ownership plan (ESOP), employees take over or participate in the management of the organization that employs them by becoming shareholders of stock in that organization. In the public sector, an ESOP can be used in privatizing a service or function. Recently, for example, the Office of Personnel Management established an ESOP for its employees who perform personnel background investigations.
Franchising of Internal Services	Under the franchising of internal services, government agencies may provide administrative services to other government agencies on a reimbursable basis. Franchising gives agencies the opportunity to obtain administrative services from another governmental entity instead of providing them for themselves.
Franchising-External Services	In the franchise-external service technique, the government grants concession or privilege to a private-sector entity to conduct business in a particular market or geographical area, such as concession stands, hotels and other services provided in certain national parks. The government may regulate the service level or price, but users of the service pay the provider directly.

Government Corporations	Government corporations are separate legal entities that are created by Congress, generally with the intent of conducting revenue-producing commercial-type activities and that are generally free from certain government restrictions related to employees and acquisitions.
Government-Sponsored Enterprises	Government-sponsored enterprises (GSE) are privately owned, federally chartered financial institutions with a nationwide scope and limited lending powers that benefit from an implicit federal guarantee that enhances a GSE's ability to borrow money in the private sector. They are not agencies of the United States but serve as a means of accomplishing a public purpose defined by law.
Joint Ventures	See public-private partnership.
Leasing Arrangements	Leasing arrangements are a form of public-private partnership. Under a long-term lease, the government may lease a facility or enterprise to a private-sector entity for a specified period. Maintenance, operation, and payment terms are spelled out in the lease agreement. Under a sale-lease-back arrangement, the government sells an asset to a private-sector entity and then leases it back. Under a sale-service contract or lease-service contract, an asset sale or long-term lease is coupled with an arrangement with the purchaser to furnish services for a specified period. Leases in which the government leases a facility (e.g., a building lease) are considered a form of contracting out, rather than a public-private partnership.

Managed Competition	Under managed competition, a public-sector agency competes with private-sector firms to provide public-sector functions or services under a controlled or managed process. This process clearly defines the steps to be taken by government employees in preparing their own approach to performing an activity. The agency's proposal, which includes a bid proposal for cost-estimate, is useful to compete directly with private-sector bids.
Outsourcing	Under outsourcing, a government entity remains fully responsible for the provision of affected services and maintains control over management decisions while another entity operates the function or performs the service. This approach includes contracting out, the granting of franchises to private firms, and the use of volunteers to deliver public services.
Performance Based Organizations	Under a performance based organization (PBO), policymaking is to be separated from service operation functions by moving all policymaking responsibilities to a Presidential appointee. The service operations are moved to an organization to be headed by a chief executive officer (CEO),[2] hired on a competitive contract for a fixed term. The CEO's contract defines expected performance and in exchange for being held accountable for achieving performance, the CEO is granted certain flexibilities for human resource management, procurement, and other administrative functions. As of March 1997, several PBOs had been proposed but no PBO had been authorized in the federal government.[3]

---

[2]GAO refers to a chief executive officer (CEO). The newest term for this position is chief operating officer (COO) as is found in the body of this report.

[3]Since the GAO publication, one PBO has been created—the Office of Student Financial Assistance Programs.

Privatization	The term privatization has generally been defined as any process aimed at shifting functions and responsibilities, in whole or in part, from the government to the private sector.
Public-Private Partnership	Under a public-private partnership, sometimes referred to as a joint venture, a contractual arrangement is formed between public- and private-sector partners, and can include a variety of activities involving the private sector in the development, financing, ownership, and operation of a public facility or service. It typically includes infrastructure projects and/or facilities. In such a partnership, public and private resources are pooled and their responsibilities divided so that each partner's efforts complement one another. Typically, each partner shares in income resulting from the partnership in direct proportion to the partner's investment. Such a venture, while a contractual arrangement, differs from typical service contracting in that the private-sector partner usually makes a substantial cash, at-risk, equity investment in the project, and the public sector gains access to new revenue or service delivery capacity without having to pay the private-sector partner.
Service Shedding	Divestiture through service shedding occurs when the government reduces the level of service provided or stops providing a service altogether. Private-sector businesses or nonprofit organizations may step in to provide the service if there is a market demand.
Subsidies	The government can encourage private-sector involvement in accomplishing public purposes through tax subsidies or direct subsidies, such as the funding of low-income housing and research and development tax credits.

User Fees	User fees require those who use a government service to pay some or all of the cost of the service rather than having the government pay for it through revenues generated by taxes. Charging entry fees into public parks is an example of a user fee.
Volunteer Activities	An activity in which volunteers provide all or part of a service and are organized and directed by a government entity can also be considered a form of outsourcing. Volunteer activities are conducted either through a formal agency volunteer program or through a private nonprofit service organization.
Vouchers	Vouchers are government financial subsidies given to individuals for purchasing specific goods or services from the private or public sector. The government gives individuals redeemable certificates or vouchers to purchase the service in the open market. Under this approach, the government relies on the market competition for cost control and individual citizens to seek out quality goods or services. The government's financial obligation to the recipient is limited by the amount of the voucher. A form of vouchers are grants, which can be given to state and local governments that may use the funds to buy services from the private sector.

BIBLIOGRAPHY

Advisory Committee on Student Financial Assistance, *The Higher Education Amendments of 1998: Meeting the Committee's New Challenges*, Briefing Document, September 1998, http://inet. ed.gov/offices/AC/ACFA/sepbrief.html#perform, 8 April 1999.

Baldwin, Laura H., Frank Camm, and Nancy Y. Moore, "Innovative Uses of Performance Metrics in Strategic Sourcing," RAND, Santa Monica, California, 1998, unpublished.

Camm, Frank, "Adopting Best Commercial Practice to the Department of Defense," briefing prepared as a course for the RAND Graduate School, RAND, Santa Monica, California, 1999, unpublished.

Camm, Frank, *Expanding Private Production of Defense Services*, RAND, Santa Monica, California, MR-734-CRMAF, 1996.

Camm, Frank, and Nancy Moore, "Strategic Sourcing: A Key to the Revolution in Business Affairs," RAND, Santa Monica, California, 1997, unpublished.

Clinton, William Jefferson, Old Executive Office Building, March 3, 1993.

Congressional Budget Office, *Controlling the Risks of Government Sponsored Enterprises*, 2, 1991.

Conant, J. B., and L. Groves, letter to J. R. Oppenheimer, February 25, 1943, Records of the Office of Scientific Research and Development, U.S. Atomic Energy Commission, Records of the

Manhattan Engineer District, 1942–48, WWII Records Division, National Archives and Records Service, Alexandria, Virginia.

Davies, Simon, "Outsourcing Big Brother," n.d., http://www. privacy.org/pi/issues/outsourcing/eds.html, 5 April 1999.

Department of Defense, *Report of the Quadrennial Defense Review*, Washington, D.C., 1997.

Eisenhower, Dwight D., Bureau of the Budget Bulletin, 1955.

Federal Benchmarking Consortium, *Serving the American Public: Best Practices in One-Stop Customer Service, Federal Benchmarking Consortium Study Report*, November 1997, http://www.npr. gov/cgibin/print_hit_bold.pl/library/papers/benchmark/1stpcus. html, 12 April 1999.

Financial Times, "Self-Assessment Working Better Than Expected," June 19, 1997, p. 7.

Gale, William F., "The Budget Gimmick of the 1990s," *Wall Street Journal*, May 3, 1989, p. A19.

General Services Administration, *U.S. General Store Description*, n.d., http:///www.gsa.gov/regions/4k/k4store/gendesc.htm, 12 April 1999.

Groves, L., *Now It Can Be Told—The Story of the Manhattan Project*, Harper and Brothers, New York, 1962.

Gunn, R., "Memorandum on Sub-Atomic Power Sources for Submarine Propulsion," memo to ADM H. G. Bowen, November 13, 1939, Records of the Office of Scientific Research and Development, U.S. Atomic Energy Commission, Records of the Manhattan Engineer District, 1942–48, WWII Records Division, National Archives and Records Service, Alexandria, Virginia.

Kane, Kimberly L., *Historic Context for the World War II Ordnance Department's Government Owned Contractor Operated (GOCO) Industrial Factories, 1939–1945*, U.S. Army Corps of Engineers, 1998.

Keating, Edward G., *Cancellations and Delays in Completion of De-partment of Defense A-76 Cost Comparisons*, RAND, Santa Monica, California, DB-191-OSD, 1997.

Keating, Edward G., Frank Camm, and Christopher Hanks, *Sourcing Decisions for Air Force Support Services: Current and Historical Patterns*, RAND, Santa Monica, California, 1998.

Kelman, Steven, *Procurement and Public Management: The Fear of Discretion and the Quality of Government Performance*, AEI Press, Washington, D.C., 1990.

Kettl, Donald F., *Sharing Power: Public Governance and Private Markets*, The Brookings Institution, Washington, D.C., 1993.

Lebron v. National R.R. Passenger Corp., 115 S. Ct. 961, 1995.

Longanecker, David A., *Statement to the Subcommittee on Post-Secondary Education, Training and Life-Long Learning, United States House of Representatives Committee on Education and the Workforce*, July 29, 1997, http://www.ed.gov/offices/OPE/announce/1997/test7-29.html, 8 April 1999.

Marcus, Alan, *Analysis of the Navy's Commercial Activities Program*, CNA Research, Alexandria, Virginia, Memorandum 92-226, July 1993.

Mintzberg, Henry, "Managing Government—Governing Management," *Harvard Business Review*, May–June, 1996, p. 75.

Moe, Ronald C., "The "Reinventing Government" Exercise; Misinterpreting the Problem, Misjudging the Consequences," *Public Administration Review*, March/April, Vol. 54, No. 2, p. 111.

Moore, Nancy, Frank Camm, and Laura Baldwin, "Strategic Sourcing: Packaging Policies and Practices of Leading Firms," RAND, Santa Monica, California, 1997, unpublished.

Moore, Nancy, Frank Camm, Christopher H. Hanks, and Paul Bricker, "Commercial Outsourcing, Patterns and Practice: Preliminary Observations from Work in Progress," RAND, Santa Monica, California, 1996, unpublished.

Moore, Nancy Y., Laura H. Baldwin, Frank Camm, and Cynthia R. Cook, *Implementing Innovative Purchasing and Supply Management Practices: Lessons from Best Commercial Practice*, RAND, Santa Monica, California, 1999.

National Partnership for Reinventing Government, "Houston U.S. General Store for Small Business," http://www.npr.gov/library/fedexec/stores/houston.html, 12 April 1999.

O'Malley, Sharon, *Partnership Strategies*, Briefing to Mary Margaret Evans, February 1999.

Pint, Ellen M., and Laura H. Baldwin, *Strategic Sourcing: Theory and Evidence from Economics and Business Management*, RAND, Santa Monica, California, MR-865-AF, 1997.

Savas, E. S., "Privatization and Productivity," in Marc Holzer (ed.), *Public Productivity Handbook*, Marcel Dekker, Inc., New York, 1992.

Smith, Marshall S., "Summary of Remarks by Marshall S. Smith Acting Deputy Secretary of Education at the Conference on The Coming Revolution in Student Aid Delivery," Washington, D.C., November 2, 1998, http://www.ed.gov/Speeches/981102.html .

State of California, *Current Status of California Base Reuse: Hamilton Army Airfield*, n.d., http://www.cedar.ca.gov/military/current_reuse/hamilton.htm#hamilton_anchor, 10 April 1999.

Task Force on Alternative Futures for the Department of Energy National Laboratories, *Alternative Futures for the Department of Energy National Laboratories*, prepared by the Secretary of Energy Advisory Board, February 1995.

Tighe, Carla E., et al., *Outsourcing Defense Services: Theory and Practice*, n.d.

Tighe, C. E., J. M. Dondrow, J. D. Keenan, A. J. Marcus, C. S. Moore, C. M. Reeger, M. T. Robinson, and R. D. Trunkey, *Case Studies in DoD Outsourcing*, CNA Research, Alexandria, Virginia, Annotated Briefing 96-62, January 1997.

Truman, Harry S., Budget Message to Congress, 1948.

U.S. Congress, Private Ownership of Nuclear Materials Act of 1964.

U.S. Congress, Postal Reform Act of 1969.

U.S. Congress, Energy Policy Act of 1992.

U.S. Congress, USEC Privatization Act of 1996.

U.S. Department of Housing and Urban Development, *1987 Report to the Congress on the Federal National Mortgage Association*, Chs. 3–4, 1989.

U.S. Government Accounting Office, *U.S. Navy/Military Sealift Command: Weak Contract Administration Led to Unsafe and Poorly Maintained Ships*, GAO/OSI-94-27, August 1994.

U.S. Government Accounting Office, *Uranium Enrichment, Process to Privatize the U.S. Enrichment Corporation Needs to Be Strengthened*, GAO/RCED-95-245, September 1995.

U.S. Government Accounting Office, *Air Force Privatization: Issues Related to the Sale or Lease of U.S. Commercial Airports*, GAO/RCED-97-3, November 1996.

U.S. Government Accounting Office, *Privatization: Lessons Learned by State and Local Governments*, GAO/GGD-97-48, March 1997a.

U.S. Government Accounting Office, *Air Force Privatization-in-Place: Analysis of Aircraft and Missile Guidance System Depot Repair Costs*, GAO/NSIAD-98-35, December 1997b.

U.S. Government Accounting Office, *Base Operations: DoD's Use of Single Contracts for Multiple Support Services*, GAO/NSIAD-98-82, February 1998.

U.S. Government Accounting Office, *DoD Competitive Sourcing: Results of Recent Competitions*, GAO/NSIAD-99-44, February 1999a.

U.S. Government Accounting Office, *Public-Private Partnerships: Key Elements of Federal Building and Facility Partnerships*, GAO/GGD-99-23, February 1999b.

U.S. Government Accounting Office, Report to Congressional Committees, GAO/ECED-95-245.

U.S. Code, Title 12, Section 1716b-23I(b).

U.S. Code, Title 12, Section 1723(b).

U.S. Code, Title 18, Section 1913.

U.S. Code, Title 39, Section 1003(a).

U.S. Code, Title 39, Section 1004(a).

U.S. Code, Title 39, Section 101(a).

U.S. Code, Title 39, Section 201.

U.S. Code, Title 39, Section 410(a).

U.S. Code, Title 39, Section, 101(c).

U.S. Congress, House of Representatives, *H.R. Report No. 206*, 102d Congress, 1st Session 114–115, 1991.

U.S. Department of Agriculture, National Finance Center, *Our Organization*, n.d., http://www.nfc.usda.gov/aboutNFC/who.htm, 14 April 1999.

U.S. Office of Management and Budget, *Circular No. A-76 Revised Supplemental Handbook*, March 1996.

U.S. Treasury Department, *Franchise West History*, n.d., http://www.ustreas.gov/franchsing/fwhist.html, 14 April 1999.

Vivar, Jonathan H., and James Reay, "Defense Working Capital Fund: The Application of the Government Corporation and Other Organizational Concepts to the Defense Working Capital Fund (DWCF)," Draft, DR901T1, Logistics Management Institute, March 1999.

Weimer, Adrian L., and Aidan R. Vining, *Policy Analysis: Concepts and Practice*, 2nd Ed., Prentice Hall, Englewood Cliffs, New Jersey, 1992.